THE YOU PLAN

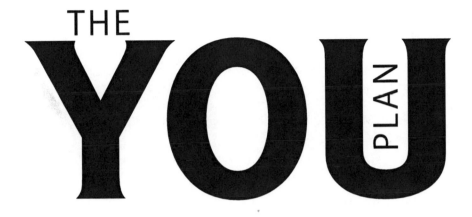

THE YOU PLAN

A **5-STEP GUIDE** *to* **TAKING CHARGE** *of*
YOUR <u>CAREER</u> *in the* **NEW ECONOMY**

MICHAEL "DR. WOODY" WOODWARD, Ph.D.

KEYNOTE
PUBLISHING
A PART OF ADVANTAGE MEDIA GROUP

Published by Keynote Publishing, Charleston, South Carolina. Member of Advantage Media Group.

KEYNOTE PUBLISHING is a registered trademark and the Keynote colophon is a trademark of Advantage Media Group, Inc.

Printed in the United States of America.

ISBN: 978-1-59932-175-2
LCCN: 2010900777

This publication is designed to provide accurate and authoritative information in regard to the subject matter covered. It is sold with the understanding that the publisher is not engaged in rendering legal, accounting, or other professional services. If legal advice or other expert assistance is required, the services of a competent professional person should be sought.

Most Advantage Media Group titles are available at special quantity discounts for bulk purchases for sales promotions, premiums, fundraising, and educational use. Special versions or book excerpts can also be created to fit specific needs.

For more information, please write: Special Markets, Advantage Media Group, P.O. Box 272, Charleston, SC 29402 or call 1.866.775.1696.

Visit us online at **advantagefamily**.com

Dedication

I'd like to dedicate this to everyone out there with the courage and tenacity to chase the American dream

Acknowledgements

I'd like to acknowledge everyone who influenced my thinking as I wrote this book (in somewhat chronological order):

My parents, Dr. James and Anne Woodward for finding a way to instill independence, entrepreneurialism, and drive in a rather awkward child

Joanne Barr for laughing at my bad jokes, providing her marketing expertise, and being a great little sister

James "Mack" Woodward, Sr. for chasing the American dream

Rick Robinson for encouraging me to pursue the field of psychology

Christian Natiello for giving me the nickname "Woody"

John Noonan for teaching me to laugh at myself

Bob Acorsi for teaching me how to have thoughtful opinions

Dr. Paul Isely for being a great mentor and comedy partner

Lynn Rae Bowen-Wentworth for teaching me to be a consultant and being a fun boss

Everett Pilson for keeping me up on my social media and being my "artist" friend

Noel Halpin for helping me find inspiration in the bottom of a "jar"

Shane M. Graber for being a true friend, painfully honest critic, and inspirational marketing guru

Dr. Nathan Hiller for being a good friend, thoughtful sounding board, and letting me graduate

Dr. David Pollack for being a good client, role model, and data provider

Fred Gonzalez for being the "Freditor" and always finding an angle

Monique "Q" Gonzalez for finding me a synonym for brand

Yolanda Harris for taking me seriously and guiding me in the right direction

Denis Boyles for instilling within me the confidence to write

Marnie Goldman for thinking to call me when the Bravo Network came looking

Tabatha Coffey for letting me come on her show and strut my stuff

The News Café in South Beach for a great little perch to do my morning thinking

The Starbucks staff at Mary Brickell Village in Miami for "office" space and cheap rent

Megan Ann Harmon for providing the "young woman" perspective, teaching me the art of "meg-storming", and putting up with me

Table of Contents

Preface

Most books of this genre start off with some sort of "this is how I got rich and so can you" tag line. I have never been big on telling people what to do because I believe that success has to come from within. You have to define success for yourself and go after it yourself.

As a coach trained in organizational psychology, I have followed the rule that you can't help those who aren't willing to help themselves. Nearly every week I come across people who tell me they want more for themselves, yet the world is somehow against them. Their past haunts them, they are misunderstood, everyone around them is incompetent, or they are just too smart for their job.

Regardless of the excuse, it always seems the circumstances are never right for these folks and probably never will be. This is a victim mentality that is not easily changed. We all know it, and some of you may even suffer from it.

After being arrested on December 1, 1955, Rosa Parks could have given up, caved to her fears, and walked away from the opportunity to turn a disturbing and tragic negative into a historical positive. She didn't. When he returned from five and a half years of routine physical and psychological torture in a North Vietnamese prison, John McCain could have easily faded away and spent the rest of his life hiding, blaming, and lashing out. He didn't. After twenty-seven years in South African prisons, Nelson Mandela could have turned his back, fled the nation that had imprisoned him, and sought refuge elsewhere. He didn't.

My point is this: We all have excuses, and the difference between success and failure is our willingness to learn from our experiences, leave the past behind, and always put the best foot forward.

This book will provide you with a method for figuring out what will work best for you. We all define success differently, and we all have different dreams. It is not my place to tell you what to want or how to be someone else. My role is to coach you in how to take charge of yourself. My hope is that you will use this book to create a personalized career plan – your very own YOU Plan – and find the success that you truly want. It's time for you to take control.

Enjoy the journey,

Dr. Woody
www.**TheYouPlan**.com

Section I:

GETTING OUT OF THE

HOT SEAT

Chapter 1

PURSUING YOUR CAREER LIKE AN ENTREPRENEUR

We have faced some tough challenges in our recent history, with layoffs, bankruptcies and foreclosures soaring. The mood has been grim as many jobs and even industries disappeared for good. Whether you are a young college student just entering the job market or a battle-tested veteran back on the job hunt for the first time in decades, the challenge has been daunting and the competition stiff. The Great Recession changed the U.S. employment landscape forever. The "new normal" has yet to be determined. The reality is we are in an era of great uncertainty.

Uncertainty is stressful, and in uncertain times, stress is everywhere. When faced with uncertainty, we have less control. Just as a horror movie will have you at the edge of your seat anxiously awaiting the next surprise, so too will the uncertainty of not knowing where your next paycheck will come from. Losing your job means losing your daily routine, schedule, and regular social contact. To some extent, you even lose your sense of identity. In essence you have lost control.

The same can be said for making that leap from college or graduate school to the working world. Fear of the unknown lurks in your mind. You have more questions than answers. You know that every choice has a consequence, yet you have no way of knowing what those consequences will be.

In either case, the uncertainty you are facing brings with it some loss of control over your life. You then start to become overrun with anxiety. That anxiety can be psychologically paralyzing, furthering your loss of control and sense of uncertainty. Whether you are a seasoned professional or a fresh face in the crowd, this book is about tackling that anxiety and regaining control through new thinking and deliberate action.

I use the hot seat metaphor on the cover (the red chair) as a way to illustrate these circumstances you are facing. The pressure and anxiety that comes from being in career transition is like sitting in your own hot seat. The future is uncertain and you know you have choices to make. The heat is on and the pressure is mounting. Recognizing that you are in the hot seat is a critical first step to taking control. By picking up this book you have taken that step. The next step is figuring out how to get yourself out of the hot seat and on a path towards a fulfilling and successful career.

As of right now, you are in the career hot seat, and it's my job to help you get out of that hot seat and back into the game. *The YOU Plan* is about discovering your entrepreneurial spirit. It's about taking the reins of your destiny.

In *Man's Search for Meaning*, renowned psychotherapist and concentration camp survivor Viktor Frankl said it best when he wrote:

> *"Man is not fully conditioned and determined but rather determines himself whether he gives in to conditions or stands up to them. In other words, man is ultimately self-determining. Man does not simply exist but always decides what his existence will be, what he will become in the next moment."*

Challenging times require creative thinking. The best way to combat the anxiety of uncertainty is to forge your own path. Throughout our history, innovative concepts and revolutionary inventions have come during the most challenging of times. Hardship and crisis ignite new thinking.

Savvy entrepreneurs look for opportunities where others have turned their backs. "One man's trash is another man's treasure," according to the old saying, and so too is one man's failure another man's opportunity. Entrepreneurs create career opportunities where they don't yet exist. The best opportunities are ones tailor-made *for* you, *by* you.

We are entering an age of entrepreneurialism, in which career success will depend on your ability to define your direction and create your own opportunities. This is the American pioneering spirit. Our nation's history is full of great entrepreneurs who fought adversity to achieve the American dream. Some of our greatest achievers thrived during times of war, recession, and personal struggle. Whether you are descended from a long line of entrepreneurial Americans or a recent entrant to our society, this spirit is part of your psychological DNA. It's up to you to activate it.

THE YOU PLAN

Whenever I work with a client who finds himself sitting in the hot seat, my first question is always: "What's your plan?" The response I typically get is an awkward pause followed by some fumbling, and then finally an admission to not really having any real plan at all. A real plan should be a coherent road map designed to get you to a specified destination. Ideas and fantasies aren't plans; they are great starting points, but they often evolve into procrastination.

I'll be the first to tell you that no plan should be too detailed and that the course you chart on your road map will never be a straight line. However, if you don't chart a course, you'll never reach the destination you want. If you want control over your life, you have to take charge. You have to make a conscious decision that you really want it. As history has shown, successful people don't wait to get rescued when they find themselves in the hot seat. They spring to action and save themselves. And they always start with a plan.

Always remember: The one variable in life that you have the most control over is yourself. My role is to provide you with a guide to creating your own destiny. I will help you take back the reins. I will help you plan for YOU.

Chapter 2

STRIKE LIKE A VIPER: YOUR 5-STEP MODEL FOR CAREER SUCCESS

I f you have been laid off, lost your business, or had your hours cut back, getting back on your feet won't be easy, but it is within your control. You need to start thinking differently. If you are coming out of college or graduate school, this is the time to start planning. You are facing a tough market with a lot of experienced competition. Whether you are 21 or 55, you have the opportunity to take control of your life by building a plan.

The YOU Plan is based on the VIPER approach. The VIPER approach is a stepped process for developing a career plan designed to help graduating students and transitioning professionals make informed choices. I created the VIPER approach to help you land that next job and embark on your desired career. It involves swift yet deliberate action. Just as a viper is quick and deliberate in its strikes, the VIPER approach will teach you to be calculated and focused in making your next career move.

The VIPER approach consists of five major components:

- **V**alues – establishing your foundation

- **I**ntrinsics – assessing what you bring to the table

- **P**assion – revisiting your ambitions

- **E**ssence (brand) – articulating your brand proposition and package

- **R**oad map – drawing out a plan for launching (or re-launching) your career

The VIPER approach teaches you how to get results by taking calculated action and striking deliberately. By helping you gain better self-awareness, focus and commitment, *The YOU Plan* will push you to create your own destiny. I want you to step back, take a breath, and seriously look inside yourself to rediscover who you are, what you have to offer, and where you want to go with it.

So grab a pen and some paper, head over to your local Starbucks (or your preferred local value option), and let's get to work!

Section II:

VALUES

Chapter 3

WHAT ARE VALUES, AND WHY DO THEY MATTER?

"Open your arms to change, but don't let go of your values."
— Dalai Lama

"Values provide perspective in the best of times and the worst."
— Charles Garfield

Taking control of your destiny requires knowing yourself. As with any personal journey, the journey of career rediscovery begins with introspection. I'm not asking you to lie down on the couch and recount your childhood pain. I'll leave that to my therapist friends. What I am going to ask you to do is think about who you are by exploring what you value.

Who you are drives how you work, play, live, and ultimately shine. Your experiences, upbringing and culture shaped the person you have become and the values you espouse. Those values influence the decisions you make and the path you follow. Your values are the lens through which you view the world. Let's begin the journey by taking a closer look through that lens.

Though values play a critical role in career choices, the unfortunate reality is that most people can't articulate their values. Often that leads to bad decisions and career paths that aren't truly fulfilling and might even be toxic. Many of you have pursued career opportunities (or even summer jobs) that ended up not being so opportune. So now you are reading this book. You are preparing to step back and consider the possibilities. First step: considering your values.

WHAT ARE VALUES?

Values can be thought of as the personal code upon which you build the foundation of your life. They are the principles that you hold near and dear and that define your character.

Webster's dictionary defines values as "… important and enduring beliefs or ideas shared by members of a culture about what is good or desirable and what is not." The Penguin Dictionary of Psychology defines values as "an abstract and general principle concerning the patterns of behavior within a particular culture or society."

When all is said and done, that which really matters to you is what you value. So, when it comes to identifying your values, the simplest exercise is to ask yourself the following three questions:

- What am I willing to pay for?

- What am I willing to fight for?

- What am I willing to sacrifice for?

The things for which you are willing to pay, fight or sacrifice are what you value. They are important to you. They are highly motivating and carry a personal meaning. Your values might include fostering a loving relationship, or attaining financial success, or staying in peak physical health. You will dedicate a substantial amount of time and energy to what you truly value. If your health really matters to you, you will spend a lot of time exercising, eating well, and monitoring your body. Maintaining a high physical standard will be a priority. Getting up at 6 a.m. to hit the gym and counting your daily caloric intake will become routine.

Many people say they value something but fail to demonstrate it. The true test is not your affinity for a particular idea or the time you spend fantasizing about it. Rather, it's the actions you take, the effort and sacrifice you make to incorporate that value into your life.

After you answer those initial three questions, you should have a basic outline of your values. Once you identify your values, it's time to put them to the test. It is now time to answer the question:

- Do I live my values?

If you don't live the values you proclaim, you have to ask yourself why. If there is a discrepancy between the values you articulate and the values you demonstrate, your articulated values are clearly not the core guiding principles that you live by. I come across many people who can speak the words, yet fail in their actions. Someone who truly values building a loving relationship doesn't cheat on his or her spouse. Someone who truly values financial success isn't perpetually broke. Someone who truly values physical health doesn't eat fast food and avoid working out.

A DR. WOODY MOMENT:

WHAT I LEARNED OVER A SAPPHIRE MARTINI

One summer evening in Miami, I was having a Bombay Sapphire martini at Drake's, the hotel bar at the J.W. Marriott on Brickell Avenue. Remembering what my grandfather had told me about the company, I asked the bartender what she thought about working at Marriott. It was the best job she'd ever had, the young woman exclaimed. "It feels like a family, and I like that. Mr. Marriott [Bill Jr.] even comes to visit us once a year."

I asked her what she knew of the hotel's heritage. In her Cuban accent, she painted me a picture of the Marriott story beginning with the A&W root-beer stand that J.W. opened in Washington, D.C., in 1927. That was the same stand where J.W. Marriott hired my grandfather.

As we talked, it became clear to me that she wasn't just reciting some training protocol. She really believed what she was saying. It had been two years since she was hired, and she could still relay the Marriott story. What struck me was the strong personal connection she had to the Marriott values. They were also her values.

To this day, you can find these core values stated on the Marriott Web site. Two in particular stand out: "A reputation for employing caring, dependable associates who are ethical and trustworthy," and "a home-like atmosphere and friendly workplace relationships."

The family atmosphere felt comfortable to her. She had found a place where her values aligned with those of her employer. This alignment enabled her to shine as both an individual and an employee. I could cite countless such examples in businesses across the country. The moral of the story is that values do matter.

I'm a realist, and I firmly believe values are about the reality of how you live. Successful people do more than talk, they do – and they continue to do until they get it right. All successful doers have guiding principles; they have clear foundational values that guide their actions.

Consider for a moment one of America's most iconic entrepreneurs, J.W. Marriott, a man who not only had a clear set of values but also lived by them. I'll never forget meeting J.W. Marriott when I was a young child. It was a warm summer day in Wolfsboro, New Hampshire. My sister and I had come up to spend a week with my grandparents at their summer rental. I was about eight years old, and my grandfather, who had been a long-time Marriott employee, had arranged for the two of us to visit the Marriott family compound just down the road.

As one of Marriott's earliest employees, my grandfather had developed a tremendous affinity for the man who had given him his first job as an adult. As a devout Catholic, my grandfather had a strong set of religious values and an almost obsessive work ethic. His values were similar to, and to some extent inspired by, his mentor J.W. Marriott, who was also a man of strong religious conviction. Because it was so important to my grandfather that I understand the value of hard work and the success it could bring, he wanted me to meet a man who he felt exemplified these values.

Shortly after arriving, we were ushered into a large living room. After we waited a few moments, an elderly man emerged from behind a door. Though he looked somewhat frail, he clearly emanated a presence that I felt the moment he walked into the room. The meeting was brief. He and my grandfather exchanged pleasantries and chatted. As we were getting ready to leave, he put his hand on my shoulder and leaned over to remind me to work hard and always treat people well.

It was a simple statement and one he had likely uttered thousands of times, but it was just the message my grandfather brought me to hear. A message he wanted me to take to heart.

The son of a Utah farmer and a devout Mormon, J.W. Marriott went to great lengths to live his values and institutionalize those values in his organization. In recounting the role of his father's values, J.W.'s son and current CEO, Bill Marriott Jr., has said that "in establishing the culture of the company, there was a lot of attention and tender loving care paid to the hourly workers. When they were sick, he went to see them. When they were in trouble, he got them out of trouble. He created a family loyalty."

Not only did J.W. Marriott have clear values, he lived them. "You've got to make your employees happy," he was quoted as saying. "If the employees are happy, they are going to make the customers happy." He made sure those values were evident in the organization he built.

He served as a great example of how clear values can act as guiding principles. According to the Marriott website, "J. Willard Marriott's life values remain the driving force behind the Marriott philosophy."

Before you can become successful in this age of career entrepreneurialism, you must identify and articulate a clear set of guiding principles. Regardless of the career or life you want to pursue, you must know and live your values. You must exemplify your values in the way you live. Your values should be evident, and you should be proud of them. I'm sure you can think of many examples of how values play a role in your career and life decisions.

To take the first step in identifying your guiding principles, answer those three basic questions posed in this section (they're also included in the values exercise in Chapter 4). For the next step, consider where your values come from.

WHERE DO VALUES COME FROM?

Everything comes from somewhere, yet figuring out where isn't always easy. Your values are rooted in your life experiences. Parents, mentors, friends, religion, culture, education, trauma – all influence what you value. The good, the bad and the ugly of your life experiences shape who you are and how you live.

It's easy to forget your roots or even deny the power of certain influences as we grow older. Often those values that we proclaim, yet fail to live, have deep roots. The further we get from those roots, the less likely we are to question them. Again, I'm not interested in playing therapist and have no intention of revisiting your childhood. Rather, I just want you to be aware of the many influences that can shape your values.

Building awareness about where your values come from will be critical in evaluating their true standing in your life and how you ultimately create your YOU Plan. As you go through the values exercise in Chapter 4, this will become evident. So, as a primer, consider a few of the major influences: upbringing, religion, and life experience.

Upbringing is certainly the base of most people's personal values. Whether you like it or not, the values espoused by your parents have a great impact on your values as an adult. At a young age, you develop a sense of right and wrong based on what your parents tell you and how you see them act. The actions they reward and punish have a great impact on what you carry forward into adulthood. One of the most noticeable sets of values we carry forward is how we treat other people. The manners and respect you demonstrate toward others are often a byproduct of your upbringing. Whether it's assisting an elderly person across the street, helping a friend clean up after a party, or sending a thank-you card after an interview, the values you develop during your formative years often stay with you for life.

We learn numerous other values-based behaviors during our upbringing, some of which can be negative and even destructive. For instance, children constantly exposed first-hand to violence and crime may develop little value for law and human life. That may lead them down a path of self-destruction. Those not exposed to education or who are brought up by parents who don't value learning may develop an aversion to formal education or going to college. They may drop out of school, limiting their ability to reach their true potential. This is not to say that you are doomed by a bad upbringing. We all have the capacity to learn and our values can change. But when assessing your values, take stock of their roots and decide whether the ones you espouse really are yours.

Another powerful influence on values is your religious and spiritual conviction. Your political views and moral standards likely have strong religious roots, even if you don't consider yourself religious – although to varying degrees, most of us grew up with some form of regular religious exposure. Some of us went to Christian Sunday school; others regularly visited a synagogue or mosque.

A primary sociological function of religion is to provide a moral code of conduct. The values taught by the many world religions substantially influence how societies and individuals act and interact. Most of the wars throughout history have been over disputes in religious-based values. Many have been rooted in misinterpretations rather than in actual differences in root values.

In essence, your religion (or devotion to a way of living) defines the standards you are to follow when interacting with those around you. Familiar values such as service to others, charitable giving, honesty, integrity, and work ethic have deep religious roots. Your stance on the death penalty, abortion, or environmental issues likely has some tie to your religious persuasion or lack of one. For most of us, regardless of perspective, religious roots are the foundation of values and must not be overlooked.

Life experience is another major influencer of values. All of us perceive, interpret, and incorporate experiences in our unique ways. As we grow, the things we see, feel and touch influence our view of the world and teach us more about ourselves. At different times in life, we tend to emphasize certain values over others due to our stage of development or the circumstances we are facing.

Serious life challenges will always test values and may cause us to question them. The key is recognizing those tests and learning from them. Most of us have experienced trauma or illness. Getting hit with the "wake-up call" can be a life-changing event. Many who face the prospect of disability or death will re-prioritize their values around health and family. It's easy to forget the power of love and support until faced with such crises. They are stark reminders of what we really value.

The experience of kindness also can shape values. If you receive charity, assistance, or random acts of kindness, you may incorporate them into your own value system. It feels tremendously reinforcing when someone, perhaps a stranger, picks you up after you have fallen or extends a helping hand during tough times. On the flip side, if you don't have such positive experiences, you may discount their role in your life.

Research conducted by Lubinski, Schmidt and Benbow (1996) demonstrated that many of our core values are formed early in life and tend to be fairly stable over time. They become second nature and often operate at a subconscious level. That is why it's important to recognize what has shaped our values – and often, the ones we espouse aren't really our own. They have a variety of origins, and you must be aware of them when evaluating yourself. It's up to you to determine what you really value and why.

WHY VALUES MATTER

Noted speaker and training consultant Brian Tracy once said that "just as your car runs more smoothly and requires less energy to go faster and farther when the wheels are in perfect alignment, you perform better when your thoughts, feelings, emotions, goals, and values are in balance." An often overlooked consideration when making career decisions is the alignment of personal values with career and work values.

A major component of any organization's culture is its values, which determine how people work together and interact with customers. The true values of a company go far deeper than a posted mission statement. They include the assumptions, reward structures, norms, and unwritten rules reinforced by leadership. Learning the values of a potential employer or business partner can give you great insight into how comfortable you will be working with them and how you will be treated, especially when times get tough.

I learned the power of values when I was in executive coach training. I was assigned a coach to guide me through the training and assist in my personal development. Coach Jim spent a number of sessions walking me through the development of my budding entrepreneurial career.

During one of our conversations, I got a bit stuck on a decision involving a partnership. I had a lot of ideas and even more potential outcomes. What I wanted to accomplish was so broad that I couldn't find a place to start. The scale of my vision rendered me helpless. I was paralyzed with inaction as I continued to stockpile ideas and potential partners to work with.

Tired of my equivocation, Coach Jim stopped me and asked: "What are your values?"

To my surprise, I struggled to articulate an answer. What I came up with was jumbled and vague. This was an eye-opening moment for me. My values were there, but I had never spent much time thinking about them, and I certainly couldn't express them intelligently. Despite all my training in psychology, I still had a hard time answering a fundamental question that plays a pivotal role in our careers and lives.

Articulating my values wasn't easy, but as I did so I began to realize just how vital my values really were, particularly when it came to decision-making. I learned that my values guide who I am, how I live, and how I prioritize my actions. By taking the time to seriously consider my values, I could direct my energy toward my most significant goals that truly aligned with my values.

Aligning your values with your goals and actions is a critical first step in building a successful career. Since that conversation with Coach Jim, I have always begun my career discussions and workshops by asking participants about their values.

WRAPPING THINGS UP

As you develop your YOU Plan, it is vital to consider the role of values alignment. First you must understand your own values, and then you must explore those of potential employers or business partners. You must seek out opportunities that align with your values.

Employment and business partnerships are like marriages. They require chemistry and commitment. Whether you are embarking on a new career or launching a venture, you are making a serious commitment. Job conflicts can have a major impact on your career satisfaction and success, so you must take the time to understand where conflicts might reside.

Any mechanic will tell you that misaligned wheels will wear your tires down quickly. A misaligned career likewise will wear on you emotionally and physically. It will ultimately take its toll on your happiness and success as well as the happiness and success of those who work with you and support you.

Any career move involves change. This change can influence your income, growth, reputation, and ultimately your future. In every career move, the stakes are high and the risk is nerve-wracking. Reconciling values can mitigate your risk.

The bottom line is this: Values do matter. So know them, embrace them, and live them.

Chapter 4

PROCLAIMING YOUR VALUES – EXERCISE I

Now that we have discussed the role of values in creating your YOU Plan, it's time to put your pen to the paper and get to work. It's important to emphasize that there aren't necessarily right or wrong values. Values are personal, and you must decide them for yourself. They aren't something you should impose on others; rather, they are a guide for yourself and how you interact with others.

VALUES EXERCISE

Identifying and articulating values is a process. Take your time and follow the steps below. At any time, feel free to backtrack to any previous step or even start over. This will take time. You will only get out of it what you put into it. If you feel you are stuck at any point, step away and come back later. You will find it helpful to refer to the previous chapter from time to time.

1) *Identify your values:* One of the most common forms of values assessment is the values checklist. Based on a review of common checklists, I have compiled a list of what I believe to be the most relevant terms used in identifying values. Review the checklist on the following page and select the top 10 values that you feel are representative of you. As you make your selections, remember to keep in mind the three basic questions posed in Chapter 3:

- What am I willing to pay for?

- What am I willing to fight for?

- What am I willing to sacrifice for?

VIPER VALUES CHECKLIST

Acceptance (belonging, tolerance)	Family (marriage, children)	Meaning (direction, purpose)	Reputation (affiliations, self-respect)
Adventure (excitement, risk)	Generosity (giving, sacrifice)	Modesty (humility)	Resilience (patience, strength)
Affluence (wealth, ownership)	Greater Good (nature, society)	Order (conformity, structure)	Respect (courtesy, gratitude)
Ambition (achievement, success)	Happiness (humor, joy)	Peace of Mind (harmony, comfort, safety)	Responsibility (commitment, reliability)
Challenge (competition, pressure)	Health (fitness, diet)	Personal Environment (location, proximity, commute)	Self Development (growth, wisdom)
Commitment (dedication, focus)	Hope (inspiration, vision)	Personal Ethics (character, integrity, loyalty)	Service (activism, public service)
Compassion (sensitivity, caring)	Independence (autonomy, flexibility)	Personal Experience (change, travel, variety)	Social Engagement (collaboration, interaction)
Competence (effectiveness, skill)	Individuality (uniqueness, differences)	Pleasure (attraction, desire, intimacy)	Spirituality (faith, morality)
Contribution (impact, progress)	Innovation (creation, invention)	Popularity (fame, notoriety, recognition)	Stability (savings, security)
Control (authority, power)	Knowledge (education, learning)	Prestige (respect, status)	Teaching (developing, mentoring)
Effort (discipline, hard work)	Leadership (influence, courage)	Privacy (personal space, solitude)	
Expression/Style (arts, culture, design)	Leisure (disengagement, relaxation)	Relationships (friendship, love, companionship)	

NOTE: For more information on values assessment, go to www.TheYouPlan.com

2) *Test your values:* It's one thing to select a bunch of values from a list, but it's another to actually spend time considering how meaningful they really are. The purpose of the next step is to put your selected values to the test. Take the top 10 values you selected and answer the following set of questions for each:

- Am I really willing to pay, fight or sacrifice to meet this value?

  Yes ☐ No ☐

- If yes, what would I be willing to pay, fight or sacrifice for this particular value?_____

- Do I truly live this value? Do I project it in the way I live and work?

  Always ☐   Sometimes ☐   Never ☐

- Where does this value come from?

  ☐ Family/upbringing

  ☐ Faith/spirituality

  ☐ Culture/environment

  ☐ Education/training

  ☐ Life experience (other)_____

3) _Prioritize your values:_ Remember, not all values are equal. You may have a greater willingness to pay, fight, and sacrifice for some values more than others. Prioritizing isn't easy, but it will help reveal what you really value. Choose the five out of your ten selected values that are most important to you based on your answers to the previous questions. Take your selected top five values and order them from 1 to 5, with 1 being most important and 5 being the least important of the group.

1)_____

2)_____

3)_____

4)_____

5)_____

4) _Articulate your values:_ Take each of your top five prioritized values and state each one in your own words. When writing your value statements, consider the following questions:

- What does the value mean to you?

- Why is it meaningful?

- How would you describe the value to someone else in a simple statement?

5) *Memorialize your values:* Now that you have identified and articulated your values, it's time to incorporate them into your career planning. Your values are the foundation of your YOU Plan. They are the principles that will guide you in serious career and life decisions. So, be sure to type up your values statements and post them in an appropriate place. Your values statements should be a constant reminder of what you stand for.

6) *Align with your values:* Whenever you are making a decision about pursuing a particular job, working with a partner, or embarking on a new career path, consider whether the choice really aligns with your core values. Ask yourself:

- Is this choice consistent with my values?

- Do the people involved (those you will be working closely with) share my values?

- By following this direction, will I be living my values?

For more information and tools for assessing values, go to: www.TheYouPlan.com.

Section III:

INTRINSICS

Chapter 5

WHAT DO YOU BRING TO THE TABLE?

"Who looks outside, dreams; who looks inside, awakens."
—CARL JUNG

*"The ultimate value of life depends upon awareness
and the power of contemplation."*
—ARISTOTLE

Taking charge and getting out of the hot seat starts with knowing yourself. At the outset of the book, I mentioned that introspection is critical in developing a thoughtful and deliberate career path. In the previous chapter, we started down the path of introspection by exploring values. In continuing this journey, I want you now to consider what I refer to as your intrinsics.

I define *intrinsics* as the assets within you. They are what you came into this world with and what you have learned since. They are what you bring to bear in every encounter, career or otherwise. Taking control of your destiny is about knowing yourself and knowing what you bring to the table.

Think of your intrinsics as a deck of cards. All of our lives are shuffled differently, which means our cards are ordered in very different ways. Some of your cards are close to the top and readily accessible, whereas others are buried near the bottom and haven't been played in a while. Knowing your intrinsics starts with throwing all the cards on the table. All too often we forget to take stock of what we have in our deck, especially when faced with the stress of making that next career step.

To build a YOU Plan and get out of the hot seat, you must take the time to seriously evaluate what you bring to the table. This section will help you explore your assets – your intrinsics – and guide you in leveraging them to build a successful career.

I have broken the concept of intrinsics into six major dimensions. You need to have a strong grounding in these six dimensions, because they are the core elements that influence the pace of your career development. I like to refer to them as your career PACERS:

- **P**ersonality

- **A**ffiliations

- **C**ontributions

- **E**xperiences

- **R**elationships

- **S**kills, Knowledge, and Abilities (SKAs)

Personality: Who Are You?

The first, and perhaps most critical, of the PACERS is personality. When it comes to introspection, understanding your personality is a key starting point. Taking back control requires knowing yourself – your natural, unfettered self. Your personality has a tremendous influence on how you function in the world – how you get along with your spouse, communicate with your boss, fit in with your team.

Whether I'm working with corporate executives or personal clients, I always begin by assessing their personality and natural strengths. I'm certainly not unique in this approach. The study of personality and its application to the world of work has enjoyed a substantial resurgence, with many theories and approaches. What's important is this: Personality does matter.

Personality researcher and organizational psychologist Bob Hogan (on his Hogan Assessment Systems website) put it this way: "Personality matters to individuals because self-understanding allows a person to be strategic about his/her career choices and career development. Personality matters to employers because knowledge about a job applicant's personality allows them to be strategic about the hiring process." The more you know about yourself, the better you can focus on the strengths of your personality.

Defining personality: Hundreds of books and thousands of research studies have explored personality and how to define it. In the business and working world, individuals want to better understand their strengths, and employers want to best predict success. So the focus tends to be on predictable traits: Employers want to know what natural inclinations match up with the successful execution of work and who possesses them.

Known as the father of "trait" psychology, Gordon Allport defined personality as a building block that shapes and drives behavior. From the trait perspective, personality is one of the behavioral drivers with which you arrive in this world, and it tends to remain fairly stable and unchanging over time. Personality is one of many drivers of behavior, though it is arguably the most significant. Others include experience, culture, upbringing, education, religion, social norms, expectations, and trauma. But your root personality can determine how you respond to those influences. It shapes how you act and interact.

Common models of personality: The most well-researched model of personality used in business is the five-factor model, also known as the big five. The big-five model theorizes that personality can be broken into five major categories or factors: openness to experience, conscientiousness, extraversion/introversion, agreeableness, and neuroticism or emotional stability. According to the model, we all have varying degrees of each factor, which combine to create our unique personality. Because the factors are so broad, most applications of the model also include in-depth breakdowns of each factor.

Empirical research has provided fairly wide support for the five-factor model across several languages and cultures. The online dating world has also jumped in the game: eHarmony uses the big five as part of its matching system, providing eager daters with customized results to help better select that perfect mate. That's right, even the folks at eHarmony feel that personality matters.

Another popular model of personality is the Myers-Briggs assessment. Originally based on the work of Carl Jung, the tool was developed by Katherine Myers and Isabel Briggs to help individuals understand and respect natural differences. Often used in team building and communication, the Myers-Briggs Type Indicator (MBTI) examines where you fall on four basic facets: Introversion-extraversion, sensing-intuition, thinking-feeling, and judging-perceiving. These four facets combine to provide 16 unique personality combinations. Over one million individuals have taken some form of the Myers-Briggs since its inception. The tool is perhaps the most popular personality assessment out there.

Regardless of the method, what's important is enhancing your self-awareness. Understanding your personality helps you identify where your natural strengths and comfort zones are. Keep in mind, we all have to operate outside our comfort zones from time to time. But by becoming formally aware of your preferences, you will know when you are leveraging your strengths and when you are straying from them. Your career pursuits should emphasize your strengths, not your weaknesses. So if walking into a chamber of commerce meeting and working the room isn't your thing, selling insurance may not be for you.

The personality assessment you use should meet a basic set of standards and provide you with valuable insight into your natural strengths – a key to career success. In the next chapter, I will give you some guidance for finding a relevant personality assessment to determine those strengths.

Affiliations: You are who you touch

What do people know about you? What do people assume about you before they even know you? Or, more simply put, what is the identity you project when you are not physically present? In life, and certainly in business, people typically know of you before they really know you. Before actually meeting you, the identity that others attribute to you typically comes from what they associate with you. In other words, your affiliations shape how you are seen before you are ever actually seen.

Often the initial information available about you will come from a website, Web search, cover letter, resume, references or friends. A potential employer or client often notices your affiliations. In his book *Relationship Marketing*, Regis McKenna talks about the importance of building credibility, product positioning, and differentiation through stronger relationships with customers. He discusses building credibility through strong and recognizable affiliations. He argues that these affiliations allow consumers to infer your credibility. By being affiliated with a particular group, company, institution, club, or association, you are sending this message: I share their values, style, experience, professionalism. I am like them, so if you like them, you will like me.

Much of our social identity is closely tied to affiliations. As part of his theory of motivation, psychologist David McClelland theorized that the human need for affiliation is powerful and involves our desires for comfort and social comparison. The bottom line is that we all need and have affiliations. We affiliate with our families, friends, employers, clubs, schools, and fraternities, to name a few.

Whether intentional or not, these affiliations all say something about us. They speak to who we are, particularly in the absence of any other information. This is why knowing and managing your affiliations is important. You must take stock of them. The company you choose to keep says a lot about who you are. As a career entrepreneur, a big part of your success will come from knowing the messages you unconsciously send.

A DR. WOODY MOMENT:
AFFILIATING FOR CREDIBILITY

When I went out on my own as a consultant, one of the greatest challenges I faced was that I was unknown. The fact that I was young and looked even younger didn't help, either – although it's been great for dating! Unlike my colleagues from established firms, I didn't have business cards with a well-known corporate logo. In effect, I had no big banner to wave that said, "Hey, look at me, I have value!" My pedigree did include the big names PricewaterhouseCoopers and IBM Global Business Services, but I was in a new town and a new market. If I was going to thrive, I had to build credibility quickly.

One reason I ended up back in Miami was for my doctoral studies in organizational psychology at Florida International University (FIU). The university had developed a great local reputation, especially in the business community. A good friend, a professor at the FIU business school, suggested that I meet with the president of the university to discuss a project they were developing. The president was interested in personality and leadership and wanted the perspective of someone in organizational psychology. He was in the midst of establishing the Florida International University Center for Leadership and wanted some help.

Knowing that Dr. Modesto "Mitch" Maidique was popular and respected, I readily agreed to meet him. As the longest sitting university president in Florida history, he had a strong presence and a passion for the study of leadership development, an area of my business that I was looking to grow. My friend arranged the meeting, it went well, and I began to work with the FIU Center for Leadership.

My first project with the center involved facilitating a session of 17 local executives, including a Marine brigadier general. In the following months, I often made reference to my interactions with Mitch and my affiliation with the center. I quickly learned that his stamp of approval meant something. In essence: If Mitch Maidique was willing to hire this kid Woody, he must know something. As of this printing, I sit on the academic advisory board of the FIU Center for Leadership. My relationships with both the university and Mitch have raised my profile and built my business.

The moral of the story is that the fastest way to establish credibility is to develop affiliations with recognizable and credible entities who take you seriously and let others know it. If potential employers or clients don't know much about you, make them feel more comfortable by showing them whom you affiliate with.

In his book *Life's a Campaign*, Chris Matthews, political commentator and longtime host of MSNBC's *Hardball,* summed up the importance of affiliations quite well:

> *"Pick your friends and bosses carefully. They are the neon lights that illuminate the way to you, that fairly or unfairly declare your character. Lie with dogs and you'll pick up fleas. Sing in the choir and they'll think you're holy."*

In building a YOU Plan, you are responsible for your own public relations. A key to successful public relations is controlling the message. As you will see in Section V (Essence), understanding the basics of how you put yourself out there will be critical to building your brand. Knowing your affiliations will ensure that you are able to leverage them in a way that sends the right message to the right audience. Remember, affiliation brings credibility by creating a sense of familiarity and connection. This credibility is what will get you past the long lines and through the tight doors.

Contributions: PAY IT FORWARD OR BUY IT BACKWARD

So much of life is about give and take. At times we give to others, and at times we take from others. We all have contributed to the world around us in some way. It may be as simple as streamlining a faulty work process or as sophisticated as winning the Nobel Peace Prize. Big or small, all of our contributions touch others, and the contributions that are positive usually have a lasting effect. As we grow, our stockpile of contributions also grows, becoming part of the intrinsics we carry forward.

A big part of what you bring to the table is what you have contributed in the past. Each of us has pursuits and pastimes on which we spend time and energy. These are things that are meaningful to us and often bring us joy. Yet, when it comes to our careers it is easy to forget about these experiences and how valuable they can be. Whether you give back to your community, help others in need, or win an award, your contributions demonstrate your values and ethics. Contributions can come in many shapes and sizes: writings, research, innovations, assistance, or changes you have influenced. Step back and assess the value you have created, and see how you can leverage that value in developing your career.

Think about what you have done for those around you. Whether you led a staff of volunteers in cleaning up your neighborhood, spearheaded a sorority fund-raiser for scholarships, or wrote for your local newspaper, your contributions have value. Consider what it took to make those contributions and what you learned by making them happen. Don't limit yourself to just considering your school work and professional contributions when assessing your intrinsics. All that you do and all that you contribute is relevant. It's just a matter of identifying, articulating, and packaging those contributions for those who will evaluate you for career opportunities.

EXPERIENCE: PACKAGE YOUR PAST

Every moment in our lives is an experience, and as we grow, we continue to stockpile experiences. The key is what we do with these experiences in moving forward. Most of the people I talk to have a reasonable grasp of their experiences, but they struggle to sell those experiences in a way that is meaningful and relevant to others. As someone who has worked on both sides of the hiring process, I can tell you that being able to package your experience is important.

Taking the time to reflect on your experiences is critical to developing an effective YOU Plan. We don't often engage in thoughtful reflection. We live in a fast-paced, urgent world, where all of us are racing toward an undetermined finish line. In his book *How Successful People Think*, author and leadership guru John C. Maxwell put it this way: "The pace of our society does not encourage reflective thinking. Most people would rather act than think." He goes on to say that "reflective thinking is the Crock-Pot of the mind. It encourages your thoughts to simmer until they're done." When we take the time to organize our thoughts, it's amazing what we can come up with. It's just a matter of stopping long enough to make sense of where we have been and decide where we are going.

In my consulting practice, one focus is on developing hiring processes for companies. This usually entails some form of structured behavioral interviewing, a technique that has become popular in the past couple of decades. A technique that I have used when training interviewers to assess experiences and behaviors is the SAR method.

A DR. WOODY MOMENT:
STEPPING BACK FOR A LOOK FORWARD

After the first VIPER workshop I conducted, I worked one on one with a few of the participants. One had been in business for himself nearly two decades and had been out of work for most of a year. He ran a specialty electronics company that did custom home installations.

As we were talking about his intrinsics, he said he was considering taking a project management class. He said he had come across numerous opportunities in the technology industry that required project management experience, and he was concerned that he lacked it.

At first I thought he just needed a pep talk but then realized he was truly unable to see the breadth of his "project management" experience. I asked him a couple of questions about his experiences with "managing client projects." As he walked me through the process of a typical installation (or project), I pointed out that he was describing the professional standards of project management, with which I am familiar.

He laughed as he realized he had actually been in project management for twenty years. He'd thought of it as technical installation and customer service. Because of his perspective and semantics, he hadn't recognized a valuable instrinsic that had been with him all along.

At times, we all fail to recognize our intrinsics. To move forward, sometimes you have to step back and talk to people who have different perspectives.

SAR stands for Situation, Action, Results. There are several variations on this concept, but the purpose is always to provide interviewers with a structure for probing candidates on their experiences. It is also a good way for you to organize your thoughts when reflecting on your experiences and preparing your own experience/interview package. The model is as follows:

Situation: For the *S* in the SAR model, I ask interviewers to look for the situation or circumstance. The point behind this is to provide context. When describing your experiences, always think first about the situation or context so as to help others understand the nature of your experience. Think about where you were working, the location, the time, the people involved, and the problem you were facing. Remember, you are telling a story. Every story starts with context. To quote the opening of my favorite space opera: "A long, long time ago, in a galaxy far, far away…"

Action: Now that you have set the context, it is time to speak to your audience about what you did. The action step is about explaining what you did specifically to address the issue you faced. This is where you answer the question, "What did you do?" Be sure to relay the steps you took in an orderly and succinct fashion so that a potential employer can understand your thought process.

Results: Now that we know the situation you were facing and the actions you took, it's time to talk about what actually came of it. We live in a bottom-line world. Employers want to know: Did your actions actually have an impact? Did your method of addressing the issue bear positive results? This is your opportunity to talk about the positive results you have produced in the past. When possible, try to use quantifiable terms. For example, metrics like percentage of errors reduced, time saved, and revenue generated are great ways to demonstrate the value of your experience and the potential you bring to the table.

Life is about learning. What you have been through and what you have taken away from those experiences is a big part of what you bring to the table. When it comes to building your YOU Plan and becoming a career entrepreneur, you must be able to talk about your experience in a way that shows obvious value to others.

RELATIONSHIPS: IT WILL ALWAYS BE ABOUT WHO YOU KNOW

You've heard it before, and you'll hear it again: It's all about who you know. Being a successful career entrepreneur requires fully leveraging your wide range of relationships. It still amazes me how many job seekers out there miss the mark on this one. It's fairly rare that I come across anyone (including employed professionals and successful executives) who fully leverages relationships, one of the most powerful intrinsics at your disposal. Successful businesspeople and entrepreneurs live and die by relationships. This is because they understand that getting things done requires people – those you know, and those you don't yet know.

When I use the term *relationships*, I am referring to relatives, friends, acquaintances, alumni, coworkers, employers, former coworkers, former employers, contacts, partners, association members, team members, club members, volunteers, and any interpersonal interactions you have had. It is a matter of stepping back and taking inventory of who is out there and how they can best help you.

Professional America is a fast-paced, work-obsessed place. So many of our contacts are fleeting, and a great deal of our time is spent being reactive. Living in this environment makes it incredibly tough to maintain a significant network of relationships or even friendships for that matter. However, relationships are the linchpin to success in the professional world, particularly for career entrepreneurs looking to get out of the hot seat – yes, people like you. The vast majority of the job market is relationship-based. Systems are run by people, products are bought by people, decisions are made by people, and ideas are generated by people. Being connected to people is a must if you want to get out of the hot seat and into the game.

We all have networks at our disposal that are far more extensive than we realize. We are in such a fast-paced world that it's easy to lose track of these valuable relationships. Keeping tabs on relationships can be tough, particularly when you leave college, grad school, or a job. Remember, proximity is one of the greatest drivers of relationships, so the further removed we become, the less contact we tend to have. It's the notion of convenience. Distance takes effort, plain and simple.

Social media websites like Facebook, LinkedIn, MySpace, Plaxo, and Ning, to name a few, are powerful tools that can go a long way towards maintaining current relationships and even rekindling old ones. I have had several former colleagues and even people who I have run into at networking events contact me through Facebook and Linkedin. Usually they end up seeking me out on these sites because the contact information they had for me was old or they simply lost my card.

Keep in mind, even the Internet can only go so far in satisfying our need for contact. We are social creatures who require physical contact. There are times when you will still need to pick up the phone and give that shout out.

So, fire up that retired cell phone you keep in the closet for emergencies, scroll through your e-mail address books (yes, all of them), flip through your dusty collection of business cards, and get those social media pages up-to-date, because it's time to start rekindling relationships. The idea is to consider who may be able to provide that extra boost or key introduction. We can be so forward-focused that it's easy to forget past relationships and the potential we have at our fingertips. Never underestimate the value of your relationships. Take the time, do some digging, and get yourself reconnected.

SKILLS, KNOWLEDGE, AND ABILITIES: YOUR TANGIBLE ASSETS

Your skills, knowledge and abilities, often referred to as your SKAs, are the intrinsics that most employers look for. They are essentially your resume highlights. The Society for Human Resource Management (SHRM) defines your SKAs as "the attributes required to perform a job, generally demonstrated through qualifying experience, education or training."

Skills: Think of your skills as what you can do – what you have been trained to do and can do proficiently. According the SHRM glossary, skill is the "ability to perform a mental or motor activity that contributes to the effective performance of a job task."

Knowledge: Your knowledge is what is stored in your brain. One of the ways in which you demonstrate and advertise your knowledge is through education, learning and certifications.

Abilities: Think of these as a combination of your unique personal talents and the capabilities you have developed over time. Human

A DR. WOODY MOMENT:
CALLER NO. 4 – LET'S TALK INTRINSICS

As a coach on a career helpline sponsored by the CBS news station in Miami, I took calls from local viewers who had been laid off or were in career transition. One caller, a seasoned gentleman, was a stockbroker nearly 17 years before he was laid off. Due to the financial crisis, he was ready to leave the industry behind, but he was unsure where to go next.

We explored his many interests and ideas, including buying a retail franchise and opening a gun range (in the background, I could hear his wife's protests about the latter). Being laid off after such a long stint had him throwing a lot of darts with no actual target. He and his family were lost and frustrated.

As we chatted about his interests, he started to realize they might not play to his strengths or align with his passions. Although he no longer liked the industry he was in, he did enjoy building relationships, connecting with people, and selling. These all seemed to bring him success. He admitted his strength was not in production and management, in which he'd initially expressed interest.

"If someone can produce it, I can get out and sell it," he boldly stated. To which I responded: Why not explore opportunities in sales? He laughed. "Selling is what I have always enjoyed," he said, emphasizing the importance of relationships.

As we spoke more, the prospects of managing a franchise or opening a gun range were not as enticing. His ability to connect and sell and his comfort with building relationships were indeed strong intrinsics. He enjoyed those aspects of work and was good at them. They energized him. He could readily leverage them.

Knowing the cards you hold in your hand and being mindful of the ones to play is critical to being a successful career entrepreneur.

resources expert and business professor Dr. H. John Bernardin defines the term *ability* as "a demonstrated competence to perform an observable behavior." For example, air traffic controllers must be able to endure a certain level of mental duress, NFL cornerbacks must be able to run a specified minimum speed, and NASA engineers must possess the requisite mental capacity to perform their duties. We all have our own unique talents and capabilities, some obvious and others hidden. It is up to us to understand what they are and how to leverage them.

Employers, business partners, and clients are always going to be interested in what you know, what you can do, and what you are capable of. Thus, both knowing and packaging your SKAs is important. As you explore your intrinsics, your task will be to articulate and translate the SKAs you have and find ways to make them relevant across different work boundaries.

WRAPPING IT UP: KNOW YOUR CARDS

Let's go back to the analogy of the deck of cards. The cards in your deck have different values and are shuffled to different positions. Some are worth more than others, and some are closer to the top and others buried at the bottom. In most any game, you must combine different cards to win. These combinations have different values depending on the game you are playing. Your choice to play a particular hand depends on the rules of the game, the cards that others are holding, and the outcome you are seeking.

It's similar when it comes to building your career. What you bring to the table are your intrinsics. You have to have a good sense of what's in the deck and what cards you have at your disposal. How you leverage your intrinsics will determine your success in building an effective

YOU Plan. Every circumstance will require a different combination of your intrinsics.

In each situation – interviews, presentations, or networking events – you must know what you bring to the table and how it's relevant. The key is to match the right combination of intrinsics to the right opportunity. Knowing your cards is a powerful and competitive advantage when it comes to getting out of the hot seat and into the career game.

Chapter 6

IDENTIFYING YOUR
INTRINSICS – EXERCISE II

In this chapter, I will ask you to take those cards in your deck of life, shuffle them, throw them down, and start putting together some winning hands. This is your opportunity to reflect on what you have, and to consider how to make the most of it. You need to build a solid foundation for creating your very own YOU Plan and knowing what you bring to the table is key.

The idea is to dig deep and think differently. I have found that many of those in transition tend to get caught up focusing on the top of the deck while forgetting about those cards that have slid to the bottom. And those of you who are about to graduate may still be struggling to identify your relevant intrinsics. In either case, take the time to consider those personality traits, affiliations, contributions, experiences, relationships, and SKAs that you may, at times, take for granted.

Each of the following exercises is designed to assist you in identifying your intrinsic assets, creating asset buckets, and developing basic asset packages. The goal is to produce a document that outlines and organizes your intrinsic assets as benefits.

A word of caution: Don't be a prisoner of your past

Our life and career experiences are so varied that it's easy to forget what we have. The unfortunate reality is that the older we get, the more pigeonholed we become. All too often I come across job seekers solely focused on doing what they have done before. Their career choices become dictated by their past and not their passions. Typically, they rely on their most recent job description or title as a guideline.

This phenomenon tends to afflict seasoned job seekers in particular, but it can happen throughout your work life. In psychology, it's called the recency effect. In the political world it's know as "what have you done for me lately". In other words, those experiences that are the most recent, or in many cases the most familiar, tend to be what we remember and ultimately, what we fall back on.

All life experiences are important, however, and it's critical that we pay homage to them all, even if they have inadvertently been shuffled to the bottom of the deck. To open doors in your career, you need to enhance your self-knowledge – and that should be liberating.

As you go through the exercises, keep an open mind and look at all the cards in your life deck. That means pulling out the jokers, deuces, and all. Depending on the game, that joker or deuce may be the wild card that gives you that needed boost. First, you have to know you have it; then, it's a matter of knowing when and where to play it.

PERSONALITY EXERCISE:

In the last chapter, we explored the role of personality and why it is so critical to know yourself. So many personality assessments are available that I certainly don't need to create another one here. Therefore, I would like to provide you with some guidance and direction in finding a good assessment that will help you build self-awareness.

Picking the right assessment: There are thousands of personality assessments out there, most of which will provide you with the same intellectual insight as taking a *Cosmo* quiz or reading your horoscope. But some are of high quality, and many of those are based on the big-five model, which we discussed, or are similar to it theoretically.

A top-quality assessment also has a rich history of rigorous testing, structure, and research support. You should get a sense of its theoretical grounding and intended applications. This is not to say you need to become an expert in psychometrics; you just need some basic awareness. There are a number of online resources, some of which are free. To check out and access some of the assessments that I currently recommend, go to:

- www.TheYouPlan.com

Also consider the following:

For undergraduate and graduate students

- Campus career center. Any good career services center will have more than just placement services but also a variety of assessment tools.

- Student services. Every school is different, but the office of student services usually provides self-development opportunities that may include assessments, mentoring, and personality workshops.

- Psychology department. Psychology programs often use personality assessments in research studies. Find out if the department will let you take some basic big-five assessments or get involved in its personality research.

For workforce veterans

- Your alma mater. Go to your alumni relations department. Often it will have programs and tools for self-assessment that you can access. I work with the University of Miami Alumni Relations Department (my alma mater) on outreach to alumni in career transition.

- Local career services offices. Local governments often have career/placement services offices designed to provide career counseling, training, and placement for citizens. These are typically taxpayer-funded, so definitely use them. For example, Employ Florida funds career services offices in counties throughout Florida. Look into government and privately funded services that may provide free assessment tools and career consultation.

AFFILIATIONS EXERCISE:

When taking stock of your affiliations, ask yourself the following questions: What am I associated with, and what does that project about me? When someone thinks of me, what do they think about? What roles do I play and where?

The following exercises will walk you through several categories of affiliations, some of which you may not have considered. The idea is to brainstorm and organize your affiliations so that you can best leverage them in building a YOU Plan.

Professional affiliations

(for each category, list affiliations you now have or once had. Don't be shy.)

Schools attended

_____

_____

_____

_____

Educational and training institutions

_____

_____

_____

_____

Professional associations

_____

_____

_____

_____

Community organizations

_____

_____

_____

_____

Government programs

_____

_____

_____

_____

Boards

_____

_____

_____

_____

Panels or commissions

_____

_____

_____

_____

Memberships

_____

_____

_____

_____

Clubs

_____

_____

_____

_____

Teams or sports leagues

_____

_____

_____

_____

Past employers

_____

_____

_____

_____

Current and former clients or business partners

_____

_____

_____

_____

Vendors and partners

_____

_____

_____

_____

Personal affiliations:

Who are you typically seen with? Who do you spend time with?

_____

_____

_____

_____

Who do you know who can open doors (think about people with connections)?

_____

_____

_____

_____

Who knows you (those with high profile and connections)?

_____

_____

_____

_____

Where do you spend your time?

_____

_____

_____

_____

What do all of these affiliations say about you?

_____

_____

_____

_____

_____

Now you must ask yourself how these affiliations influence how others see you. You must assess the extent to which these affiliations precede you. In others words, which affiliations do people tend to know about or recognize before or when they meet you?

Understanding how others see you through your affiliations will help you to better craft and control the message you put forth in your career search. This will be particularly important when you get to the Essence (brand) section. Knowing what you project is part of building your brand as a career entrepreneur. Your affiliations say a lot about you, whether you realize it or not. So, when you jump out of that hot seat, you'd better know what people are going to see.

CONTRIBUTIONS EXERCISE:

The following set of questions is intended to get you to think about your contributions. The questions are fairly wide-ranging and in some cases may seem repetitive. Don't feel obligated to answer every question. The idea is to spark your thinking. Take your time.

Professional contributions:

What have you given to fellow employees/colleagues?

_____

_____

_____

_____

What have you given to employers/business partners?

_____

_____

_____

_____

What have you given to clients and/or customers?

_____

_____

_____

_____

What have you been recognized for professionally (by employers, associations, schools, government…)?

_____

_____

_____

_____

What awards have you received professionally?

_____

_____

_____

_____

Community contributions:

What have you given to your community?

_____

_____

_____

_____

What have you given to those in need?

_____

_____

_____

_____

What have you been recognized for in your community?

_____

_____

_____

_____

What awards have you received from your community?

_____

_____

_____

_____

General contributions:

Who have you helped?

_____

_____

_____

_____

What change have you set in motion?

_____

_____

_____

_____

Where have you made a difference?

_____

_____

_____

_____

Who have you touched and impacted?

_____

_____

_____

_____

Experience exercise:

In the previous chapter I introduced the SAR method as a useful tool for sketching out your work experiences. What I want you to do here is consider work situations where you had tangible success. Think about those work/personal experiences and interactions where you faced tough challenges and were able to produce good results. Break these experiences out into the SAR categories and refine them to the point that they are simple and easy to understand. The SAR method is a great way to prepare for interviews, especially behavioral interviews. Remember, the purpose here is to tell a story that connects with your audience and conveys your potential.

List at least five of your major past experiences that you think make you a valuable asset as an employee, consultant, partner or entrepreneur.

1)_____

2)_____

3)_____

4)_____

5)_____

SAR method: Break each of the above major experiences out using the SAR method. Remember to keep it simple and top-line. You want to be able to tell the story quickly.

Situation: What was the situation? For each of the five experiences, describe the situation? What was the problem that needed to be solved? Where were you? What were you doing? What was your mission/ purpose?

1)_____

2)_____

3)_____

4)_____

5)_____

Action: What were the actions that you took to tackle the problem? For each of the five experiences describe the steps you took. What was your thinking process? How did you go about taking responsibility and action? What is it that YOU did?

1)_____

2)_____

3)_____

4)_____

5)_____

Results: What was the outcome? For each of the five experiences describe the results that your efforts produced. What impact did your actions have? Did you solve the problem addressed in the *Situation* part?

1)_____

2)_____

3)_____

4)_____

5)_____

Relationships exercise:

Nearly every aspect of life revolves around relationships. However, many of us take our relationships for granted and even let our valuable relationships lapse. Maintaining and continuing to build relationships is a critical element to both personal and career success. When re-engaging in your career, you must assess your relationships.

Personal relationships:

What relationships do I have that I can leverage?

Family

_____

_____

_____

_____

Friends

_____

_____

_____

_____

Neighbors

_____

_____

_____

_____

Acquaintances

_____

_____

_____

_____

Classmates

_____

_____

_____

_____

Professional relationships:

Coworkers

_____

_____

_____

_____

Colleagues

_____

_____

_____

_____

Associates

_____

_____

_____

_____

Other relationships:

Fellow members (clubs, associations, sororities, fraternities, sports, schools, faith-based organizations…)

_____

_____

_____

_____

Like-minded people (people who have similar interests, aspirations, and causes that you may not really know all that well, but should.)

_____

_____

_____

_____

Re-engaging:

When you look through these lists ask yourself the following questions:

- Am I effectively leveraging these relationships?

- Who do I need to get back in touch with?

- Who can help me get connected to people I need to meet?

<u>S</u>KILLS, KNOWLEDGE, AND ABILITIES EXERCISE:

Skills:

Most of us have a pretty good handle on what we have in our arsenal. But consider those skills that you may have let go over the years and may need to revisit as you start thinking about developing your YOU Plan.

Relevant skills I currently possess and have mastered:

_____

_____

_____

_____

Skills that I used to have and probably need to brush up:

_____

_____

_____

_____

Alternative names for these skills. (People outside your industry may call your skills something else. How would you explain and sell these skills to someone who doesn't know much about them? Remember, part of your job is to teach others about you.)

_____

_____

_____

_____

Alternative applications. (Where else can these skills be applied? Think unconventionally.)

_____

_____

_____

_____

Knowledge:

Quite simply, the question here is this: What do you know?

What credentials or certifications do you have?

_____

_____

_____

_____

What training have you been through?

_____

_____

_____

_____

What reading and self-learning have you done?

_____

_____

_____

_____

Abilities:

Ability is primarily about talent. It's about those special talents you have and those unusual things that come naturally to you.

What are your abilities? What comes naturally to you? What are you capable of that sets you apart from others?

_____

_____

_____

_____

Where can you apply these abilities as a career entrepreneur? How can you use these abilities to set yourself apart?

_____

_____

_____

_____

At this point, you will have made progress in taking stock of what you have. As you move forward, keep the following in mind:

- Don't be a prisoner of your past; embrace it and learn to leverage it – all of it.

- Know your deck of cards. Learn to pull out your intrinsics from your experiences and use them to your advantage.

- Use the right jargon or industry terminology to describe your value to potential employers or partners.

- Define your value proposition in the new economy. In other words, how do you want to define yourself? How do you expect others to view you and the value you bring to the table?

Section IV:

PASSIONS

Chapter 7

WHAT DO YOU WANT TO BE WHEN YOU GROW UP?

"I didn't want to repeat my parents' life. I saw in their lives a routine and a lack of dreaming, a lack of the possibilities, a lack of passion. And I didn't want to live without passion."

— HUGH HEFNER

"In business, I loved cars. I couldn't wait to get to work in the morning. Only in America can you decide to get a good education and pursue what you like."

— LEE IACOCCA

What do you want to be when you grow up? Every one of us was asked this question as children, whether by a pesky grandparent or a teacher. You probably gave a variety of answers, depending on your favorite TV show or most recent field trip. The inquiries seemed tongue-in-cheek, yet their intent was noble: to spark your thinking.

Throughout your formative years, many of your experiences served to excite your imagination and inspire your thinking. You were free of the constraints and obligations of adulthood. Every day brought new possibilities. Dreaming was the norm, not a luxury. Most of your days were spent fantasizing about what could be.

As you grew older, your path became more defined. Elementary and high school provided structure and grounding, a foundation for learning. The process of discovery became prescriptive as courses were selected for you, and the possibilities became more limited. College required picking a major, a general choice for your life direction. These choices provided select options designed to guide you toward a pre-determined set of career opportunities. Then, graduation necessitated finding a job, a means for surviving in the world. For many of you, this is the reality you are facing right now as a college senior or new graduate. What choices do you have, what choices can you make, and what path should you follow?

Even for my more seasoned readers, those choices still guide you, and in some cases, they haunt you. As your early career choices took hold, your work life began to take precedence, becoming a defining force in all that came later. As time progressed, your track became narrower and the possibilities you once pondered as a child faded as your responsibilities mounted. Career, for many, became more a way of life than an opportunity for expression.

For most of us, our paths narrow as we grow older. Most career-track American professionals attempt to follow a somewhat linear path designed to slowly step them toward industry seniority and retirement. Although we may not always realize it, every choice we make plays a part in this narrowing path. It is easy to get locked on a track, do what you are told, and hope for an uneventful ride. The more focused you get, the more you tend to let go of your dreams, interests and true passions. Everything becomes a means to an end, and your passion fades.

In this chapter, I want you to stop for a moment and consider where you are and why. My goal is to push you into thinking about where your passions truly lie and why aligning your passions with your career pursuits is so important. Remember, the key to getting out of the hot seat and becoming a career entrepreneur is taking control of your life. It is about the enthusiastic pursuit of career success on your own terms. That's right, *your own* terms. Granted, that which excited you as a ten-year-old may not be where your passions lie these days, yet the question of passion is more relevant now than it ever was when you were a kid. Now the answer has real ramifications as you are sitting in your career hot seat urgently trying to come up with answers.

As an adult, it is up to you to create your own choices and call your own shots. You now have the power to pursue the passions you once dreamed of. No parent or counselor now tells you what you can and can't pursue. Sure, you have more responsibility, but that responsibility is your choice. How you deal with it is up to you and no one else. If you are willing to take on the responsibility, face the risks, and make the tough decisions, your passions can be yours.

What do you want to be when you grow up? In more adult terms, the question might be rephrased as: What are your passions? What are your ambitions? What will bring fulfillment to your life?

A DR. WOODY MOMENT:
HIRING FOR PASSION

After I'd conducted a workshop at a community college job fair, the college's public relations director asked me for an interview. Her question was simple: "Can you give me some tips I can publish in our newsletter?"

I told her I'd like to talk about how important it is for job seekers to identify their passions and demonstrate them to potential employers. She wasn't interested, she said abruptly. "I need tips that will actually help – who cares about passion?"

I pointed out the large turnout of job seekers in the hall and reminded her of the 10 percent unemployment level. Every employer, I said, has lots of choices, and a nice resume and polished interview script aren't going to cut it in a "buyer's" market. "If the folks lined up in this hall want a shot," I said, "they are going to have to differentiate themselves."

Overhearing us was the former vice president of recruitment from a major national car rental agency. He asked if he could comment. "I'd love to get your comment," the PR director responded, ready to take notes. He looked at her. "I've been in the recruitment business for 15 years, and if you don't show me passion, I won't hire you." Turning to me, he commented, "Some people really just don't understand that we are in different times." I shook his hand, smiling at the PR director.

Conventional thinking is hard to overcome. Some people just want a simple answer so they can be on their way. If you have made it this far in the book, you definitely aren't one of them. Keep seeking out those passions.

PASSION AND MEANING

Passion often has been linked to the pursuit of that which is truly meaningful. In *Man's Search for Meaning*, Viktor Frankl tells of surviving Auschwitz and Dachau by relentlessly pursuing a sense of meaning. As a prisoner, he spent much of his time trying to make sense of the tragedy surrounding him and helping his fellow prisoners get through each day.

"There is nothing in the world, I venture to say, that would so effectively help one to survive even the worst conditions as the knowledge that there is meaning in one's life," he wrote in his book. His passion for finding meaning in life enabled him to emerge from the death camps and find success as a psychotherapist, ultimately starting the movement known as Logotherapy. His life and work provide insight and inspiration on the power of passion.

Understanding what is meaningful to you personally is a critical step toward finding your passion. There is no right or wrong answer to the question of what your life means. What is personally meaningful is different for all of us. To find your own sense of meaning, ask yourself questions such as:

- Why do I think I'm here?

- What do I want to achieve?

- What do I want to contribute?

- How can I influence others?

- What can I do to leave this world in better shape than when I got here?

- What makes me happy?

Any superstar has a story and a reason for pursuing greatness. On the NFL pregame show on any given Sunday, you'll be sure to find a story of passion, meaning, and success. You'll hear how a player came from desperate circumstances and triumphed by relentlessly following his passion for the sport. Passion and meaning are within your reach, too. It is up to you to discover them – and to align them with the passions of those around you.

PASSION AND CORPORATE CULTURE

The culture of an organization consists of the values, philosophies, assumptions, and norms that drive its collective behavior, business theorist Edgar Schein explains in his book *Organizational Culture and Leadership*. Quite simply, the company's culture dictates how people act and interact and what's appropriate. That's why it is critical that you understand the culture of any potential employer or business partner. You will spend most of your waking hours working, so you need to find or create an environment where you can channel your passions effectively.

Two examples of passion in corporate culture can be found in Zappos. com and Green Mountain Coffee.

The Las Vegas-based online retailer Zappos.com, which Fortune magazine included in its 2009 list of 100 Best Companies to Work For, has ten commandments to guide its culture. The ninth is "be passionate and determined."

"We do our best to hire positive people," founder and chief executive officer Tony Tsieh said in a Fortune magazine article. He went on to say that they strive to "…put them in an environment where positive thinking is reinforced."

The Zappos.com culture is one of open creativity and free expression. Its human resources team asks candidates questions designed to probe their inspirations and passions. At Zappos.com, passion and a positive attitude are not only encouraged, they are a requirement to get hired.

Green Mountain Coffee, based in Vermont, has been ranked five times on the Forbes list of Best Small Companies and was an HR Magazine choice for Best Places to Work. One of the core values stated on its website is: "Passion for coffee – From tree to cup. We roast great coffees and are committed to ensuring that everyone who encounters Green Mountain Coffee has an outstanding coffee experience." The folks at Green Mountain Coffee clearly respect the role that passion plays in producing and delivering a top-quality product.

Green Mountain even has a program called Community Action for Employees, or CAFE, in which employees can take paid time off to engage in community service passions of their choice. By doing this, Green Mountain acknowledges that not all passions center on work. The CAFE program is way to help enrich the lives of both its employees and the community it relies upon.

An organization's culture, as you can see, is powerful and dictates the extent to which passions can be expressed. Your success and happiness will depend upon a good fit with an employer or business partner. When developing your plan and exploring potential employers, consider these questions:

- Are my passions aligned with the mission of the organization?

- Does the culture of the organization support the pursuit and expression of my passions?

- Will I enjoy the work?

- Will I be engaged in the work?

- Will I be willing to go that extra mile?

- Will I be satisfied with my contributions?

Good companies and smart recruiters care about passions. Living your passion is tremendously satisfying, and satisfied employees create a healthier and more harmonious work environment.

PASSION AND ENGAGEMENT

Passion is often what tips the scale in hiring or choosing a partner or client. Those who are considering working with you want to know whether you truly have a passion for the work. They will want to see that you have that inherent energy and drive to create best-in-class products or provide top-quality service. Their biggest questions will be: Does your motivation and enthusiasm come from within? And can it be harnessed? In this new age of the career entrepreneur, competition will be fierce. Employers want those who stand out as wanting to be there and giving it all they've got.

Over the last decade or so, consultants and academics have given much attention to the concept of employee engagement – whether the worker demonstrates genuine interest and enthusiasm. Many businesses are plagued by "presenteeism," which is when employees go through the motions but aren't truly engaged and become unproductive. They just show up and punch in.

Why would you want to spend most of your day as disengaged as a zombie? Employers, partners, customers and clients all want to see passion emanating from you in all that you do. Would you want to stroll out onto the soccer field with a goalie who didn't really feel up to playing for your team? The same goes for your career. If you aren't in the game and you aren't there to do it right, think about the kind of message that sends about you as a person. Who wants to play with a loser or even be around one?

Watching the clock is no path to success. It's only a path to the next day. To build a successful YOU Plan, you need to be engaged. Engagement begins with passion. Without passion, you will never get out of the hot seat and make it happen.

PASSION AND SUCCESS

Many of the world's top achievers have found their success through the pursuit of passion. And by success, I'm not solely talking about wealth. When I talk about success as a career entrepreneur, I'm really talking about finding personal fulfillment and having control. In other words, doing what you want to do. Only you can define your success. But however you do, your passions will be a guiding force in how successful you become.

In 1984, when Frankl updated his preface to *Man's Search for Meaning*, he wrote: "For success, like happiness, cannot be pursued; it must ensue, and it only does so as the unintended side-effect of one's personal dedication to a cause greater than oneself or as the byproduct of one's surrender to a person other than oneself." Whether you seek to be the best in your business, make a lasting mark, or save the world, be sure you have a true passion for it. Whatever your cause, passion will always be the foundation of your success.

CASE IN POINT

KATE SPADE: A GIRL'S PASSION FOR HANDBAGS

Kate Spade went from a relatively low-paying position as a fashion and accessories editor to award-winning designer and entrepreneur. At Mademoiselle magazine, she spent her days writing about and reviewing the designs and successes of others. That is, until her boyfriend (and future husband) persuaded her to step out and pursue her passion for design. Although worried about her lack of training and experience, she decided to let her passion guide the way.

Kate Brosnahan and Andy Spade built a multimillion-dollar business out of Kate's passion for handbags, fashion, and sense of etiquette. Today, the subsidiary of Liz Claiborne has 46 shops worldwide and a number of retail partnerships. "Based on Kate's love of textiles, pattern, and strong geometric shapes," the Kate Spade website says, "the company developed a signature, iconic design element."

The pursuit of passion can open doors you never knew existed. Who would have ever thought this young magazine editor would end up building a fashion empire.

Aaron Patzer, young entrepreneur and founder of Mint.com, created his software as a solution to his need for a simple way to track personal finances. In a 2009 interview, Inc.com (the online version of Inc. Magazine) asked him about his decision to sell Mint.com to software giant Intuit.

"I thought about what I really love to do," he responded, "and what I love to do is build things." He continued on to say: "I've been doing that since I was six years old, with Legos."

Patzer's success with Mint.com came from his passion for building something new, something that solved a problem. For him, success wasn't as much about the $170 million sale (although a very nice perk) as it was about the possibility of his solution reaching millions of Americans. Although he planned to stay on with Mint.com during the transition, the article noted he was already looking forward to his next venture.

When you have passion, your inner drive pushes you forward even when you are worn down. You know you have begun aligning with your passions when you wake up in the morning raring to go and ready to jump. Life starts to feel effortless. This is not to say you will be able to strike perfect alignment between your passions and career pursuits, but there is no reason not to close the gap, or at least try.

WHY PASSION MATTERS

Show me a truly successful professional who doesn't wake up every morning excited to get to work. Show me a great athlete who doesn't exude passion, one who didn't grow up dreaming of being on the field or stepping out on the court. If you take a moment and think about what sets these people apart, you'll typically find that it's passion. We can all come up with examples of success stories, those who live the dream – and all of us have our own dreams and aspirations, but it's that underlying passion that really matters.

We all need food, shelter, and water to survive. We all need love and support to get by. But these should be the means to a greater end. If you focus career efforts on meeting immediate obligations – on surviving – instead of feeding your passions, you will never truly thrive. As we get older, we tend to become jaded, some faster than others. The best way to avoid that is to keep your passions alive.

A WORD OF CAUTION: HARNESS YOUR PASSION

It's important to recognize that the term *passion* can have negative connotations such as "impetuous" and "ungovernable" that serve to emphasize passion's potent emotionality. The news is full of graphic headlines about "crimes of passion" in which love affairs turn to obsession. And we have all seen passion in activism go too far. All too often people push their views so forcefully that they do more damage to their cause than good. Passion can be powerful – sometimes too powerful.

Your goal, of course, is to leverage your passions as a strength and minimize any liability. Passion is not license to disrespect, demean, or attack those who don't share your views. You want to harness your passion for personal and professional gain. You must focus your passions in a positive and constructive way.

WRAPPING IT UP

To leverage your passions as a career entrepreneur, you need to draw on your natural enthusiasm. When you find a career pursuit that lets you channel your passions, success will be inevitable. So, let's get back to my opening question: "What do you want to be when you grow up?" It's really about what excites you. What generates enthusiasm? What makes you want to leap out of bed in the morning? Keep in mind:

- Your passion is what drives you when all of your other motivators fail.

- Your passion is what sets you apart when all else is equal.

- Your passion is your own.

Don't be afraid to explore your passions. Getting out of the hot seat will require focus and enthusiasm. Let your passion be the catalyst for your future success.

Chapter 8

REDISCOVERING YOUR PASSIONS – EXERCISE III

To rediscover passions, you need to ask yourself some questions. Reflecting on your past isn't easy. I recommend that you work with a partner when going through these questions. Sometimes having to explain your answers out loud to someone else is a good way to really test how meaningful they really are.

Your childhood dreams:

What did you want to be when you grew up?

_____

_____

_____

Why? What inspired those dreams?

_____

_____

_____

Do you still have passion for those dreams?

_____

_____

_____

Are there still opportunities here?   ☐ Yes   ☐ No
If yes, what are they?

_____

_____

_____

Your positive experiences:

What were some high points in your life? Think about times when you really felt in your groove or felt as if you had strong, smooth flow in getting things done. (Consider past jobs, community events, school, classes, leisure activities…)

1)_____
2)_____
3)_____
4)_____
5)_____

Why were they high points? What made those moments memorable?

_____

_____

_____

What are the common themes of these experiences?

_____

_____

_____

How do these experiences relate to your values? Did your values play a role in these experiences?

_____

_____

_____

What are the opportunities in these high points? How can you revisit them? How can you leverage the common themes for future success?

_____

_____

_____

Your inspirations:

What inspires you? Where do your ideas come from? (Think about what gets you excited or generates enthusiasm.)

_____

_____

_____

What gets you out of bed in the morning? (Besides your blaring alarm!)

_____

_____

_____

_____

What makes you feel whole – as if you have accomplished something worth accomplishing?

_____

_____

_____

_____

Where are the opportunities here?

_____

_____

_____

_____

Your passions:

In light of your previous answers, what are your passions? What do you really enjoy that still piques your excitement and sparks your interest?

_____

_____

_____

_____

_____

_____

In which of these areas are you willing to test the waters? In other words, which three passion areas do you think you may be able to consider pursuing?

1)_____

2)_____

3)_____

Chapter 9

ALIGNING YOUR VIPS – EXERCISE IV

This book is called *The YOU Plan* because it's about you. You are your number one VIP (Very Important Person), and up until this point you have been focusing on what I will now refer to as your VIPs (Values, Intrinsics, and Passions). Now that you have had the opportunity to reflect and make some decisions, it's time to align them into a "VIP matrix," a cohesive vision for harnessing your essence and creating a road map (the next two sections of the book).

THE VIP MATRIX

For each of your values and intrinsics, select your primary five. These are the top five values that are most important to you and the top three intrinsics that you feel you have the best handle on (or you feel are your best assets).

	Values	**Intrinsics**
List your primary five values and primary three intrinsics	1) _____ 2) _____ 3) _____ 4) _____ 5) _____	1) _____ 2) _____ 3) _____

Passions

	1)	2)	3)
List your primary three passions			
List the values and intrinsics that best align with making each passion become reality	_____ _____ _____ _____	_____ _____ _____ _____	_____ _____ _____ _____

Emerging themes: What are the major themes you see emerging across your VIPs? What jumps out at you when you look at the matrix?

_____

_____

_____

Note: Be sure to take some time on this one. Also, share the matrix with your spouse or a friend to find out what themes they see.

THE YOU VISION

In light of your VIPs, it is now time to determine your vision. Think about what your VIP matrix says to you. Your vision is the big picture of yourself. It's your aspirational view of who you want to become and what you want your career and life to look like.

What do you want your career to be about?

_____

_____

_____

_____

What do you want your life to be about?

_____

_____

_____

_____

What is your vision for you? What do you want YOU to be about?

_____

_____

_____

_____

SETTING YOUR DIRECTION

Based on the emerging themes, select two career directions you feel strongly that you might pursue and that align with the VIP matrix. For each of the two directions, think about the relevant VIPs that you will need to draw upon to make them happen. The relevant VIPs may or may not be in the matrix, and it's OK if they are not.

*1) First career direction*_____

Relevant VIPs

Which values support this direction?

_____   _____

_____   _____

_____   _____

Which intrinsics will be critical in supporting this direction?

_____   _____

_____   _____

_____   _____

Does this align with my passions and if so, how?

_____

_____

_____

_____

2) Second career direction_____

Relevant VIPs

Which values support this direction?

_____   _____

_____   _____

_____   _____

Which intrinsics will be critical in supporting this direction?

_____   _____

_____   _____

_____   _____

Does this align with my passions and if so, how?

_____

_____

_____

_____

Section V:

ESSENCE

Chapter 10

LEVERAGING YOUR ESSENCE

"A brand is a living entity – and it is enriched or undermined cumulatively over time, the product of a thousand small gestures."
– MICHAEL EISNER

"And I'm not an actress. I don't think I am an actress. I think I've created a brand and a business."
– PAMELA ANDERSON

T aking control over your career destiny is about claiming ownership and letting everyone know it. Just as lawyers will tell you that possession is nine-tenths of the law, I will tell you that perception is nine-tenths of reality. In other words, you are what you project.

The previous three sections focused on taking stock in yourself, the essence of who you are. The exercises encouraged you to dig down and uncover the building blocks of who you are and what you are about.

But your VIPs – values, intrinsics, and passions – will help you only if people know about them. Now it's time to take those building blocks and create a brand package that you can use to launch you out of the hot seat and into the market.

WHAT IS YOUR ESSENCE?

When I speak and give workshops on the VIPER process, I often tell participants that if they can answer the question, "What are my values, intrinsics, and passions," they have virtually answered the question, "What is my essence?"

Essence comes from the Latin word *essentia*, meaning "what it was to be." The word's origins are rooted in attempts to translate a concept of Aristotle's often thought of as concerning the soul, according to the Stanford Encyclopedia of Philosophy. It appears Aristotle felt that everyone has some form of an inner-core or foundation. His point: There is more to you than meets the eye.

French philosopher Jean-Paul Sartre talked about a man's essence as being self-determined or created throughout the tenure of his existence. In his 1946 lecture *Existentialism is a Humanism*, Sartre stated that "man is nothing else but that which he makes himself." Although that is contrary to many religious interpretations of essence (in the sense of soul), he was saying, simply, that your choices affect your experiences, which come to define the life you live. In other words, the values you espouse, the intrinsics you develop, and the passions you embrace are the foundation of your essence – at least in the earthly sense of the word.

The tough questions you already have answered have helped you uncover those foundational blocks. Now it's time to start building.

Understanding your essence is one thing, being able to effectively project it out to the world in a way that benefits you is quite another. This is where branding comes in. It's time to create a package that represents and projects your essence. It's time to build your YOU brand.

PACKAGING YOUR ESSENCE

To take control and live your life deliberately, you need to build your own brand as a career entrepreneur. Harnessing your essence is about building a brand and marketing your assets.

Every product you encounter has been deliberately packaged, displayed, and positioned to be sold to a particular audience. Many times that audience is you. Now it's your turn to be the marketer. This is your opportunity to take your essence and turn it into a marketable package for the world to consume.

As you navigate the rest of this chapter, please keep your VIP matrix handy as a reference. Many of the concepts that I will be presenting here will require referring back to your VIPs for guidance.

Consider these five steps as you work toward building a YOU Brand:

- Audit your brand

- Craft your message

- Speak like a politician

- Be your own pimp

- Live your brand

1) Audit your brand: Before you can begin building your brand, you need to get a sense of its current state. How do those who know you see you? Remember, you don't know what you don't know. It's a simple fact, yet one that eludes many: Knowledge that you don't seek is knowledge that you don't have. So it's time to start asking some questions.

In the marketing world, the notion of checking yourself is called the brand audit. Typically, good marketers begin their projects with a briefing based on a brand audit. The idea is to understand the work that lies ahead. In the coaching world we call this a 360-degree assessment, which entails surveying colleagues on major areas of competence and character to get an outside perspective.

When I have used 360-assessments in the coaching process, I often find that clients are a bit surprised by the results. The reason for this is quite simple: We are all victims of living in our own heads.

Shane M. Graber, vice president and brand managing director of Grey Goose Vodka, candidly told me that "as marketers, we have to be careful not to believe our own hype." In other words, be mindful of your blind spots. It's easy to lose touch with how the outside world views you. To avoid this, Graber recommends a thorough brand audit to assess the current state of your brand, as seen by the consumer.

Graber also emphasized that what's important is not just how you see yourself, but also how your audience sees you. There is no doubt that auditing yourself as a brand isn't easy. You need thick skin. However, the benefits can be tremendous. By asking hard questions and taking the tough criticism, you open yourself up to really learning about how others perceive your brand and what adjustments you need to make.

Take the time to sit down with close friends and colleagues to get some feedback. When considering whom to ask, think about people who will be straight-up with you. This isn't about validating your own thoughts, it's about learning the truth. The only opinions of real value are going to be the honest ones, the ones that get a little under your skin and make you feel uncomfortable. When seeking feedback:

- Be open and receptive

- Don't be defensive

- Ask questions (always seek clarification when needed)

- Listen and learn

- Say thank you!

Your brand audit is about gaining intelligence. Expect to hear some surprises. Take what you hear in stride and be willing to build on it. Once you have a sense of where you are, you can begin thinking about which of your VIPs aren't getting out there and where you need to focus as you craft your message and build your YOU Brand campaign.

2) Craft your message: In building your YOU Brand, you need to boil down your VIPs into a simple and digestible message that is true to you. There are four things you need to do:

- Be positive

- Be focused

- Be relevant

- Be unique

Be positive: It signals confidence and a good attitude. Particularly during challenging times, you don't want to be seen as a downer. Downers just drag everyone down with them. Maintaining morale can be tough, so no employer wants to bring in a poison pill.

When creating your brand message, focus on what you *are* as opposed to what you *are not.* Focus on being positive and true to yourself. While crafting your message, think about stickiness: What is it about your message that will stick in someone's head the way a catchy pop song will haunt you for days? Whenever you see a TV ad, drive by a billboard, or close down a pop-up ad, pay attention to what sticks with you. Reflect on what it is that you remember. Usually, the successful messages are ones that convey how your life can be made better by using the advertised product. Successful brands are usually pitched as positive solutions. People want to feel good and thus want to know what you are going to do to meet that end.

Be focused: Casting a wide net is a common mistake. You can't be all things to all people. I once came across an independent consultant who claimed to be a "jack of all trades" – and he even added "and master of none." Prior to that statement, I didn't know what he offered. After that statement, I no longer cared.

The less specific you are, the more undefined you are. When it becomes difficult to slot you, you aren't memorable and you certainly aren't very credible. Your value proposition has to make sense and stick in the minds of your audience.

Think about how you make your own choices when spending money. I doubt you'd ask your family physician to do heart surgery. You would likely want to see a specialist with expertise and experience in fixing hearts. Consider your favorite restaurants. What is the atmosphere, what are their specials, what are they known for, and why do you go? More often than not, you go with the brand you know. By focusing, you create a brand that is known for something specific, and something sticky.

It's fine to expand your reach as you grow, but it all starts with focus. Know your niche and stick to it. Be the specialist who has a solution designed to meet defined needs.

Be relevant: In their 1980 classic *Positioning: The Battle for Your Mind*, noted marketing gurus Jack Trout and Al Ries talked about the notion of positioning in marketing consumer products. As a career entrepreneur seeking to get out of the hot seat and create your next career opportunity, you are in an increasingly crowded world where change is the norm. In building your brand, you have to be relevant.

To be relevant, you need to connect with your audience and fulfill a need. You must be aware of what others are seeking and the role you can play in helping them get there. When dealing with customers or bosses, ask yourself one question: "What can I do to make their lives easier?"

Being relevant is about providing actual solutions to current problems. In creating your YOU Brand, position yourself as a solution provider, someone who meets specific needs and does so better than anyone else.

Be unique: Relevance is not enough. In *Differentiate or Die*, which Trout coauthored with Steve Rivkin, the simple premise is you need to stand out to demonstrate value. Trout and Rivkin talk about the challenge of creating a Unique Selling Proposition (USP) in today's global market. Originally proposed by legendary marketing guru Rosser Reeves, the USP is about embracing and promoting brand uniqueness. For our purposes, it's about leveraging your VIPs to demonstrate your value proposition to potential employers, partners, or clients. It's demonstrating what you bring to the table and why you stand above the rest.

In an increasingly competitive global marketplace, access to goods and services is becoming much easier. Even when meeting a relevant need, your value proposition is going to continually become less and less unique because your competition is now more available, thanks to the World Wide Web. Jobs are being shipped offshore, and what was traditionally face-to-face work is now being done via webcasts and Skype. As your space gets more crowded, you will have to continually work at tweaking your message and demonstrating what differentiates you.

As you craft your brand message, think beyond just what you offer; think about your special twist and the audience you are going for. You must be thoughtful and deliberate. "When crafting a brand message," Graber told me, "you must clearly understand how your audience will receive that message—and ensure that the message is suitable. Remember, when Chevy launched the Nova in Mexico, they neglected to realize that 'no va' means 'no go' in Spanish. ... This was a poorly crafted message."

Successful branding requires articulating why you are the better option and letting others know about it. Use your VIP matrix as a foundation for creating a positive, focused, relevant, and unique brand message.

3) Speak like a politician. Once you have crafted your message, wrap it up and put a nice bow on it. Before you walk into any situation, you'd better know more than just what to say; you'd better know how to say it. Every good politician knows his or her talking points. You, too, need to develop your set of talking points.

Every opportunity to get your brand message across will likely be fleeting, so you need to make it count. With the proliferation of on-demand communication, every moment seems precious. We truly live in an ADD nation. The new reality is that you need to have your message down to a couple of quick sound bites or it likely won't be heard.

"In the online world of texting and tweeting, messages need to be short and simple," Joanne Barr, director of marketing for the boutique jewelry maker Stella & Dot, told me. If you want to be heard, you must be focused – "in the cluttered marketplace, you have but mere seconds to catch a consumer's attention." As a competitor in the on-line world, this is something Barr knows all too well.

Those talking points, as the sound bites are referred to in politics, are simple statements that get the message across neatly and cleanly. They have three major components: credibility, value proposition, and differentiation. In crafting your talking points, I recommend that you take your newly crafted message, break it down into simple sound bites, and then ask yourself these questions:

- *Do I establish credibility?* Do your talking points quickly show your experience or background? This is your chance to offer some current or past affiliation that will signal your credibility. Think about experiences with known companies, specialized education, and credentials.

- *Do I demonstrate my value proposition?* Do your talking points show your relevance to meeting people's needs? Do they demonstrate what you bring to the table? Think about what you do or offer, your knowledge of the industry, and similar problems you have solved.

116

- *Do I stand out?* Do your talking points show your Unique Selling Proposition (USP) and why you stand out from the rest? Do your talking points grab your audience and say, "I have a better way"? Think about your special skills, unique training, proprietary systems and processes, and your innovative perspective.

Your talking points should come across naturally. Even if you don't want to sound prepared, you had better be prepared, just as comedians practice their punch lines. "I'm just preparing my impromptu remarks," Winston Churchill once was quoted as saying as he worked on an address — meaning, of course, that no remarks should ever be impromptu.

Experienced politicians know the importance of talking points. What separates the truly masterful ones from the rest is the ability to weave their talking points into every interview answer and conversation. "It is a rare politician indeed," political commentator Bill Press wrote in his book *Spin This!*, "who would appear on television or hold a news conference without talking points."

4) Be your own pimp: I mean this tongue-in-cheek, of course. You don't need a fur coat and a fluffy hat, but you do have to sell your wares. This is called brand amplification — getting out there and being heard.

In my talk with Graber of Grey Goose Vodka, he offered this perspective on brand amplification:

> *"You can have the highest quality product, the most beautiful packaging, the most phenomenal benefits, and the most appealing performance, but if nobody is aware of the brand,*

you won't sell a unit. In today's world, you need to carefully determine how you can get the word out about your product. Whether through PR, advertising, social networking, the Internet, etc., you have to get it out there."

So take control. You are the product. You have a package to sell, so get it some attention. Specifically, consider how you can leverage social media, build a network, and be shameless.

Leverage social media: Social media is an ever-changing phenomenon, and it can be tough to keep up with. Currently, the most popular sites include FaceBook, YouTube, Twitter, MySpace, LinkedIn, Ning, and Plaxo. Beyond these sites there are also a multitude of specialized sites focused on particular industries, vocations, regions, and interests.

Potential employers, partners, clients, or even acquaintances likely will search online for information about you after meeting you for the first time. It will be up to you to decide on the message they see. To control the message, you first must know what's out there that comes up in the search engines, and then you must take the time to review the information to make sure it's current, appropriate and consistent:

Current – Is your information up-to-date, and does it reflect your brand? Are you projecting yourself the way you want to be seen now and tomorrow? Get rid of old content, particularly if it's irrelevant to your current pursuits or inconsistent with your VIPs. Your message needs to project who you are now and where you are looking to go.

Appropriate – Do the pictures and content on your sites and pages represent the image you wish to project? Keep your audience in mind. Know what they expect and appreciate. Your content needs to connect with your audience and make them feel comfortable with you as a brand.

Consistent – Is the information consistent on all the public sites? It is easy to lose track of where you have information posted and who has access to it, but all the channels through which your message is expressed should be aligned. The social media are powerful tools that can provide excellent brand amplification. However, if your message is contradictory, you could do more harm than good.

The bottom line is to maintain a consistent brand message rooted in a solid set of talking points. And use common sense. If it's on the Net, it may be seen by far more people than intended. So if those keg stand pictures or your Girls Gone Wild photo shoot aren't as flattering as they once seemed, you may want to pluck them out of cyberspace before they become a permanent fixture on someone else's site.

Build a network: As a consultant, I have spent a lot of time at lunches, association meetings, networking events, fund-raisers, happy hours, and so on. When I started my consulting business, my father joked that all I did was arrange and go to lunches. As I was working to get my business going, that was in fact pretty much the case. Being in a new town, I arranged as many lunch and coffee meetings as I could to get that valuable one-on-one face time with local players. In his book *Never Eat Alone*, former marketing expert Keith Ferrazzi talks about the value of using those meal-time moments for making genuine connections. Ferrazzi focuses on techniques for sparking relationships and cultivating new ones, so as to get your brand out there. As I learned first-hand, not eating alone is a powerful tool.

When I arrived in Miami I also spent a lot of time at networking and community events. Being a social guy in a social town like Miami, I

A WORD OF CAUTION:
PEEK-A-BOO, EVERYONE SEES YOU

As you test the boundaries of social networking, be mindful of how you use these tools and who else has access to them. All too often I come across excessive oversharing and mindless postings that could have grave ramifications. Ask yourself who really needs to know that you just stubbed your toe or have a hangover from doing too many shots last night. It's solely up to you to decide what you want to share and how much attention you need. However, pay attention to who else has access to your public musings and the extent to which they may prove harmful in your career search.

Remember, anything you post on the Net is fair game for friends and recruiters alike. Your presence on the Web will shape how you are viewed. Do a quick search for yourself and see what you find. You have to know what is out there, where it came from, and what it says. Brand continuity is important, and the nature of your presence on the Web is critical in determining your brand continuity. Be sure the messages that you send – and that others send about you – accurately represent your brand, as defined by you.

realized events were going on constantly. You never know whom you will meet and where it will lead you. You can introduce yourself to people you would not normally come across via the Net or in your usual daily activities, and it's a great way to practice your communication skills. The more diverse the range of events you attend, the broader your network will become.

Networking isn't just about getting to know others; it's also about getting others to know you. Socializing isn't networking. Socializers may be good gabbers but have no real purpose beyond the joy of chatting. Any networking you engage in has to have a strategy, defined goals, and tangible outcomes. You want to build a presence in your professional circles, the local business community, and the community at large. Your goal is to get your name out there in front of those who matter. Networking is about building awareness by creating connections. And those connections should open doors to opportunities.

Before going to any type of networking event, consider the outcomes you are seeking. Tangible outcomes may include business cards, contact information, or invitations to connect. To prepare yourself, ask yourself the following questions:

- Why am I going?

- Who are my targets?

- What is my message (talking points)?

- What do I expect to accomplish?

- How will I know this was a successful event?

- What will be my next steps?

Networking is powerful partly because every person you connect with has his or her own network. Each has links to other networks with endless potential. Whenever someone in your network comes across an opportunity that matches your expertise, your name should be the first one to come to mind – that is, if they know your talking points and value proposition. In a sense, you should be developing your own cadre of passive recruiters.

Let me repeat: It's all about who you know. You have to put in the effort. Although there are fantastic social networking and Web media tools out there, nothing can substitute for good old-fashioned person-to-person networking. The connections you can make through interpersonal interaction are powerful. In a world where opportunities are increasingly sparse, having a large network to fall back on can be a tremendous advantage. We all take comfort in familiarity. As Grey Goose's Shane M. Graber pointed out earlier, we tend to go with the brands we know. Deliberate and thoughtful networking is a path toward becoming a known brand.

Be shameless: The YOU Plan is about *you*! A critical element to your YOU Plan is creating and promoting your YOU Brand. In other words, you are going to have to actively engage in self-promotion. Getting out of the hot seat is about finding alternative routes and taking them.

Sometimes you will have to be a bit shameless as you take control and present yourself in a way that accurately reflects who you are and what you have to offer. Every step discussed in this chapter will help you do that. I want to be clear: Being shameless doesn't mean being a hack. The branding process is very deliberate. The reason I spend so much time on the assessment and articulation of your VIPs is to make sure you are ready for primetime.

This is not to say that you need to run around making public appearances or banging pots and pans. Not everyone is an extrovert; if you tend to be introverted, I'm not asking you to change. There are a lot of ways to promote yourself. Some of them are more shameless than others, and some require more energy. Think about what avenues work best for you, and focus on those.

A DR. WOODY MOMENT:
BEING PRESENT

With the proliferation of instant communication, much of our social contact is fleeting. Between all the texts, instant messages, tweets, e-mails, telepathy and mind-melds flying around, it's a wonder we ever actually speak to one another anymore. During networking events and team building, one of the greatest challenges I face is lack of engagement. In the yoga world, this is referred to as being present.

At networking events, people often will start a conversation with me and then jump on their BlackBerries, all while asking me for help. Not only is it rude, it demonstrates a serious lack of presence. If you want my time, you need to give me yours, and you'd better give me a reason to care.

Selling the YOU Brand means connecting emotionally. When you are engaging with others and trying to get a point across, show that you care and are paying attention. Having a relevant and unique selling proposition is a great start, but it's not enough. You have to actually communicate it to your audience in a meaningful way that is heard and respected. That requires being present.

Setting down your mobile life communication command center for a moment won't result in mass destruction and loss of life. You aren't that important. So, when engaging with others, shut it off and pay attention. Be respectful. If you are a slave to your BlackBerry or iPhone, you are not in control. In the new economy, no one wants to hire a robot.

For those who are more outgoing, your energy likely comes from connecting and engaging with others. If this is you, hiding at home and surfing the world of social media isn't going to cut it. You need to get out, find out where the people are who have the opportunities you want, and go for them. For example, if you are looking to develop a career in the human resources profession, start going to local HR professional groups, happy hours, and conferences. Going to these venues will give you one-on-one access to the people who have successfully built the career you want. Seek them out, approach them, convince them of your value, and learn all that you can. If you find that to be energizing, then by all means get out and hustle.

Speaking is also a great way to get your message out. Often, local professional groups, community organizations, and chambers are looking for local experts to present on particular topics. The same is true for national organizations that may use webinars to reach out to their membership. Any organization that is in the business of providing information is always looking for quality content. Consider your message, package it for your audience, and find an avenue to deliver it.

For those of you less comfortable with socializing, spend time leveraging social media or arranging one-on-one meetings with prospective mentors. Working the room isn't for everyone, so take a more intimate approach to reaching out if that suits you better. Arrange lunches and coffees with those willing to spend the time. Don't ever be afraid to ask. When I moved to Miami, I approached executives and even local celebrities about doing lunch. More often than not they said yes. If you don't ask, you'll never know.

Also consider leveraging your expertise in ways that will get your message to large audiences without the stress of actually being in front of large audiences. Often, professional associations and academic institutions will host webinars, blogs, and chat rooms designed to discuss topics in your field. Use these opportunities to provide your perspectives.

When I use the term *expert*, I don't mean to say you have to be a Nobel Prize winner or renowned theoretician. Remember, you are presenting to your peers. Your role is to provide your perspective based on your own experiences. And, it's your chance to give it your own unique twist. Find out where you need to be to get in front of the right crowd.

Whether in-person or online (or, ideally, some combination of both), take the talking points of your brand and put them in front of those who need to see them. Get on the radar screen of like-minded people who can help your career. Always be sure to present a simple, clear, and consistent message that is focused, relevant and unique.

For some, this process will be more uncomfortable than it will be for others, but it must be done. Others besides yourself need to know who you are and what you offer. Don't shy away from getting in the game, because awareness is half the battle. The brand that people know is the brand they are going to hire.

Advertising pioneer and campaign consultant Rosser Reeves was a believer in delivering genuineness through simplicity and repetition. His heavy reliance on simple repetitive slogans back in the 1940s and 1950s is still good form today. Reeves believed that what a candidate stands for has to fit on a bumper sticker. Part of being shameless is the willingness to get out and continue to deliver your talking points as often as you can, until they stick. So ask yourself: What does my bumper sticker say?

5) Live your brand: If you want to create and sustain an effective brand, you have to live it. Your brand should be projected in everything that you do. As Graber advises, awareness of your own brand is critical and always starts with a brand audit. In other words, you need to get some feedback on how others see your brand to make sure that it truly represents you. Consider the following questions:

- Do you truly project your brand?

- Do people see it?

- Do people get it?

CASE IN POINT:
BIG BERTHA: DARLING OF THE GOLF WORLD

Ely Callaway, founder of Callaway Golf Co., understood differentiation. Not only did he produce a unique golf club, he also gave it a quirky name. Targeted toward amateur golfers, the oversize driver Big Bertha took the golfing world by storm in the early 1990s.

Not long after its release, the Big Bertha became the most popular driver on the Senior PGA and LPGA tours and in 1994 became the number one driver on the PGA tour. Both Annika Sorenstam and Phil Mickelson have won tournaments playing with Callaway's Big Bertha drivers.

The unconventional club gave millions of golfers the boost they so badly wanted, and it had a memorable name. At the height of Big Bertha's popularity, it seemed most every golfer had Callaway's cannon in his or her bag. His product stood out from the competition and offered a unique golfing experience. He differentiated his product and did it proudly.

In a game of ego like golf, who wouldn't want to kick-off every hole with a stand out drive. And, what better way to stand out in consumers' minds than having a unique and memorable brand that delivered on its promise.

When I talked about knowing your VIPs I focused on the importance of introspection. Introspection is key to understanding the essence of your brand, but it's not enough. Equally important is making sure that you project your essence, so that those around you receive an accurate picture of who you are and what you represent.

"Noise," as the word is used in the study of interpersonal communication, is anything that obscures your message as it is being transmitted – the manner of presentation, consistency of message, style of delivery. If your essence doesn't translate into a brand that your audience perceives accurately, you have noise. Noise comes from lots of places, and it's up to you to figure out how to best quiet it by projecting a consistent brand message, without distraction.

Your brand isn't communicated just through your talking points. It's also communicated through the way you live. For our purposes, living your brand refers to flashing your style and walking your talk.

Flash your style: I'm not big on following convention when it comes to wardrobe advice. I'm a guy who wears boots with my suits. Rather, I believe that you are dressing for success when you are sending the message you actually want to send. This requires knowing your VIPs, having a coherent brand, and projecting that brand effectively.

To dress for success, you must show consistency between the brand you talk about and the brand you look like. You have to go with what works for you and not the general population. Here are some things to consider: fit, respect and style.

In her book *Change One Thing*, image consultant Anna Soo Wildermuth states: "Good style has nothing to do with expensive clothes. A $50 shirt can look as good as a $250 one if it has the right fit." When it comes to clothes, regardless of your style preferences, fit is key. Don't just dress how you like; also dress to your body. Both men and women can have custom clothes made for very competitive prices. You just need to research your options.

I now have my suits and dress shirts made by a personal tailor (Tom James Co.), and it made all the difference in the world. Every time I wear one of my custom suit combinations, I get complimented and I love it. When your clothes fit right, you just feel better. Looking good not only sends the right message, it is a huge confidence booster.

You also need to show respect in how you dress. Be mindful of your environment. In every situation, take note of your surroundings. Pay attention to the culture of the organization and the parameters it has set for dress and self-expression. Respect the traditions of those you intend to work with and be around – at least early on.

This is not to say you need to mimic the attire of your mentor or potential boss (often a mistake), but do understand the rules of the game. Once you earn your lumps, you can think about breaking out. Don't be flashy just for the sake of it. My rule is that if you are going to break the rules, know what they are first and have a good reason for doing so.

Style is a big part of how you project your brand. "It's about projecting your essence in a way that is visible and credible to others," according to Stella & Dot's Joanne Barr. "In other words, your look has to be your own." Before you can project your style, you must decide what your style is and put it out there in a deliberate way.

Guys in particular struggle with this. Believe me, I know, as my mother and several past girlfriends can attest. Ladies have their troubles, too.

However, women tend to consult one another for fashion feedback. That's a good lesson for the men: Don't be afraid to ask how you look. Women also have a wider variety of style options, but that comes with a higher level of expectation, especially from other women. Diverse options and high standards are good, but there's more chance of inconsistency.

We all have likes and dislikes. What's important is that you align your preferences with what you are trying to project and that you look good doing it. Pay attention to your wardrobe and spend some time thinking about what really works for you. You should ask yourself (and your friends) the following questions:

- What amplifies my essence (without causing distraction)?

- What enhances my brand message?

- About what do I typically get compliments?

- What works for me? What looks and feels right?

Always consider what has worked for you and what hasn't. If your current style (or lack thereof) hasn't worked well for you, then change it. Clear out the closet and fill that donation bag. Change is a good thing. I do believe in stepping out and taking risks as long as it's done thoughtfully. Experimenting with new looks can be fun and even informative. It's another chance to learn more about yourself and gauge reactions. Your job is to determine what's acceptable and, within those parameters, carve your own niche.

Walk your talk: When I say we all are victims of living inside our own heads, I mean we all have a unique perspective — we know things about ourselves that others don't — but we don't always transmit it effectively.

LIVING HER BRAND – BEING RACHAEL RAY

When it comes to living her brand, Rachael Ray is a stellar example. The genuinely charming TV foodie quickly captured the hearts of millions of Americans with her raw and uncensored style. A large part of her appeal is her ability to connect with her audience in a very honest way.

In an age where media personalities are so obsessed with unrealistic body images, it's no wonder that viewers and readers appreciate Rachael Ray's sincerity. In a 2007 interview with People Magazine the Food Network star was asked about her concerns with weight and her response was "I don't deny myself. I don't want to be a size zero that badly." Anyone who spends as much time talking about, preparing, and enjoying food as Rachael Ray would be a bit disingenuous if she didn't admit to enjoying the fruits of her labor. It would be hard to imagine taking cooking tips from an obsessive dieter worried more about the latest fashion than the sizzle on her stove.

When People Magazine asked Ray about her success she responded "It's very important to me that everything is accessible. People love that sort of friendly advice and that sense of community when you get advice from a peer instead of an expert." As a multimillionaire entrepreneur with four shows, 13 best selling cookbooks, a national magazine, line of cookware, and her own brand of extra virgin olive oil (or EVOO as she would call it) she has remained amazingly true to herself and accessible to her audience.

There is no doubt that this media darling has parlayed her genuine passion for food into tremendous success by very deliberately being herself. She is who she is and she is consistent about it both on and off the camera. Rachael Ray truly lives her brand.

On the flip side, the perspectives we believe that others have, are, for the most part, created within our own heads. Everything we read and hear is filtered by our own minds. Therefore, our thoughts and opinions about others are always somewhat tainted by our own perspectives.

Therefore, consider that not everything about your essence and brand gets out the way it should. My point is fairly simple: Mind the gap. That is to say, look for the gap between what people actually know about you and what they need to know about you. Closing this gap is critical to ensuring that you are seen as walking your talk. In closing this gap, don't be afraid to seek feedback from those who know you best.

And consider another gap you may need to close: doing what you say you are going to do. A big part of branding is making a promise. Every brand promises to deliver something, and your ability to deliver is what can make or break your brand. We have all been around big talkers only to be disappointed when they don't deliver, fall flat, or just can't get it done. Walking your talk is delivering on your brand promise. Don't be a talker unless you plan to be a doer as well. Ask yourself the following questions:

- What do people think of me?

- Do people have the right impression of me?

- Am I consistent in doing what I say? If not, where am I inconsistent?

- Do I walk my talk?

Your talent and value may not be readily obvious, so make sure you project it as best you can. Also, be sure to do what you say and be who you are. Once you have feedback from a few of your friends and colleagues, think critically about the adjustments you need to make to ensure you are accurately projecting your brand.

Inconsistency creates noise. The same goes for those who try too hard to stand out. When your look, actions, and affiliations become the focal point of what you project, you have to be mindful of the actual message you are sending vs. the one that is being received. If the way you live becomes a distraction, ask yourself how much of it is true to your essence and how much is just mindless noise. Pay attention, be critical of yourself, seek feedback, and work on being good at being you.

WRAPPING IT UP: YOU ARE YOUR OWN MARKETER

We all spend a great deal of time both consuming and representing brands. Whether you are just grabbing a Starbucks on campus or buying your second car, you are very aware of the brands you consume. The same can be said for your college and career life. Whether it's the university you attend or the company you work for, you probably spend more time than you realize representing that brand. Chances are you are quite familiar with the slogan, mission, and selling points. Who doesn't know their school mascot or company tag line?

But do you know your own? It's likely that you have spent very little time pitching and representing yourself as a brand in the true sense of the term. Times are changing, and to get out of the hot seat you will need to make that shift.

The job market is ever-changing, so you have to make sure that you are always positioned correctly. Branding is a deliberate process. You always have to be *you*, but you must present yourself in a way that is relevant and in demand. At the end of the day, it's your reputation, your career, and your brand.

Chapter 11

CREATING THE YOU BRAND – EXERCISE V

N
ow that you have a good handle on your VIPs, it's time to think about how to leverage them to put your best foot forward. You are the owner of your brand, and it is up to you, as a career entrepreneur, to control the message and image you project.

1) AUDIT YOUR BRAND: CHECK YOURSELF

As your own marketer, you create an image and a promise that is consistent, sustainable, and meets a particular need. Before you can work on building your brand, you need to assess the current status of your brand. A successful YOU Plan must be grounded by a strong brand. To begin the process: self-assess, test reality, and revisit your VIPs.

Self-assess

Status:

What am I about?_____

_____

What am I known for?_____

_____

What is unique about me?_____

_____

What is the promise I make?_____

_____

What is the brand I project (what do others see when they see me)?___

_____

Execution:

Do I deliver on the brand promise I project?_____

_____

_____

Do other people get what I'm trying to project? Do they see what I want them to see?_____

_____

Test reality

Once you have answered these questions for yourself, test the waters and find out what others think. The purpose here is to examine your own assumptions and look for discrepancies. Pick out a couple of trusted friends, classmates, or colleagues and ask the following questions:

Positioning: How are you positioned?

- What do you think of when you think of me?

- What do I represent?

Value proposition: What do you bring to the table?

- What do I offer?

- What problems do I know how to solve?

- How am I helpful?

Distinction (USP): What makes you stand out?

- What makes me stand out?

- What makes me special?

- What do I bring to the table that is different from my competition?

Based on the answers to these questions ask yourself: What is the brand I really project? Take some time and write out the themes that you are consistently hearing from your family and friends when it comes to your brand. Be honest with yourself and take a hard look at the differences between what you believe you project and what others tell you that you project.

_____

_____

Revisit your VIPs

Does the brand you project align with your VIPs? Do you live and project your values and passions? Do you effectively leverage your intrinsics?

- Do I project my values (can others see them)?

- Do I project my passions (do others know about them)?

- Do I project my intrinsics (do others know what I am capable of)?

If you answer "no" to any of those questions, ask yourself why. Look at your VIP matrix and think about how to best communicate your essence and brand. Take stock of yourself and ask if you effectively project who you are to those who matter.

The whole point of the brand audit is to ask yourself: Do I project the brand I believe I project and want to project? If your answer is no, go back to your VIPs and really think about what you want your brand to be.

_____

_____

2) CRAFT YOUR MESSAGE

What are you about? Based on your vision and the two directions you identified in creating your VIP matrix, determine your niche, value proposition, and differentiators. These may differ for each of the two, so repeat the exercise as needed.

Niche: What is your niche? What is your area of focus or specialty? What do you call it?

_____

_____

_____

_____

Value proposition: What is your value? What do you offer? What do you bring to the table?

_____

_____

_____

_____

Differentiators: What makes you special? What makes you unique? What makes you stand out?

_____

_____

_____

_____

3) SPEAK LIKE A POLITICIAN: DEVELOP YOUR TALKING POINTS

After you create your message, you must create a set of talking points that support your message. Talking points should be simple and to the point. You may want to create a few distinct sets of brand talking points tailored for different audiences.

Credibility: What recognizable affiliations, accomplishments, or experiences do you have that support your message? What simple fact will provide instant credibility? Think about something that connects with those in your audience, that indicates you have what they are looking for. Consider past employers, former clients, degrees, certifications, credentials...

_____

_____

_____

_____

Value proposition: Look at the value propositions you identified earlier and figure out a way to best articulate them. Be sure to keep your message in mind. Consider the following questions: What do you have to offer? How do you solve their problem or make their pain go away? What do you bring to the table that enhances their position or brings benefit? Why would someone want to hire or work with you?

_____

_____

_____

_____

Differentiators: Look at the differentiators you identified earlier and figure out a way to best articulate them. Again, keep your message in mind. Consider these questions: What makes you stand out from the competition? Why are you a more interesting choice for meeting their needs? Why are you the better option?

_____

_____

_____

_____

Finalize your talking points: Outline your talking points and commit them to memory.

_____

_____

_____

_____

4) BE YOUR OWN PIMP: AMPLIFY YOUR BRAND

Make sure you drill your talking points into the heads of those who really need to hear it. Your job is to develop an army of passive recruiters. To accomplish this, you will need to choose a number of ways to get your message out. In the previous chapter I focused on social media and networking.

Leveraging social media: Social media are a powerful force. Identify opportunities for each item in the following list. Think about content, audience, and venues. With blogging, for example, what knowledge and expertise can you offer, who is looking to learn from what you know, and is there a particular association, news outlet, or Web site you could blog for?

- Blogging_____

- Chat rooms_____

- Discussion boards_____

- Social networking sites_____

Using the social media, you must be current, appropriate, and consistent. Look at how well your messages on the social media are aligned with your brand. Ask yourself the following.

Are my social media outlets:

- Up-to-date?

- Appropriate and representative of who I am?

- Targeting the right audience?

- Under my control?

- Aligned and consistent in the messages they project?

- Sending the message I want to send?

Building a network: Nearly every city or town has many business and community groups that meet regularly to link people together. Networking groups offer more than just the opportunity to meet new people. They also offer you the opportunity to present, volunteer, or engage in skill building. In the list below, identify networking opportunities:

- Networking groups_____

  _____

- Professional associations_____

  _____

- Clubs and social groups_____

  _____

- Chambers of commerce_____

  _____

- Happy-hour groups_____

  _____

- Community organizations_____

  _____

- Charities and fund-raisers_____

  _____

5) LIVE YOUR BRAND:
WHEN BEING YOU, BE DELIBERATE

Enjoy being you and letting others know who you are and what you do. Live your brand. Look at how you project yourself and consider any tweaking that may be necessary. The key areas to focus on are *flashing your style and walking your talk.*

Flash your style: Take a long look in the mirror and ask yourself: Do I look good? Then look in your closet and ask yourself:

- How old is my wardrobe?_____

- Does my current wardrobe really send the message I want?

  _____

- When was the last time I cleared out some of my older work clothes?_____

- Do my clothes really fit me well?_____

- What can I replace or get rid of?_____

Your wardrobe is an investment in your brand. Whatever your style, be sure to own it. Consider what you want to project. Be thoughtful, deliberate, and make some donations to your local Goodwill or Salvation Army.

Walk your talk: When someone asks you what you are about, you'd better have a crisp and concise answer that grabs their attention and makes a lasting impression. Then, you'd better be sure you can back it up with action. If you ever want to be taken seriously, you will need to do what you say. Before making a commitment, always be sure to ask yourself:

- Can I really do it?

- Do I really want to do it?

- Will I actually do it?

Your brand is a promise. If you can't deliver on that promise, your brand won't hold up. Your brand is more than just projecting an image, it's being that image. Make the promise, keep the commitment, and live your brand.

Section VI:

ROAD MAP

Chapter 12

SETTING A COURSE: THE YOU PLAN

"It's hard getting somewhere without a map. It's the same reason so many of us love biographies."
– Chris Matthews

"The one with the plan is the one with the power."
– John C. Maxwell

L ife is uncertain, and recent history is a stark reminder. It's easy to take what we have for granted and even easier to fall prey to contentment. Change is the one true certainty, and the only way to navigate the challenges of constant change is through preparation. In other words, you'd better have a plan, and it needs to be flexible.

This chapter is about the value of planning and why having a road map to your future is critical to career success. Every good road map will show a number of alternate routes. To get to your destination, you will likely have to use some back-up routes from time to time. There are no straight lines to any of life's destinations.

To varying degrees, we all know how to plan, whether for a test, a meal, a vacation, a work project, a date, or a garden. Yet we rarely expend a lot of energy on planning for the big stuff. And it's even rarer that I come across anyone who plans for a career in a meaningful way. We are good at planning the short-term stuff, but not the long-term stuff.

Long-term planning isn't easy, but it is the foundation for success in any endeavor. If you want career success, you have to plan for it. It's really that simple. Before we get to the actual planning exercises in the following chapter, I want to spend a little time talking about the value of planning and share some prominent views on the subject.

SET YOUR VISION

Every plan starts with a vision. You have to see the dream before you can make it happen. You have to know what the destination looks like before you can find a way to get there. Whether you are just graduating from college or launching a business you have to start with a vision.

In business vision is everything. Successful executives are often thought of as visionary. Their ability to overcome the constraints of conventional thinking and see possibilities gives them that extra edge. According to Dr. Nathan Hiller, professor of management and a fellow at the Florida International University Center for Leadership, most leaders who are truly visionary "know who they are first." They have a strong sense of their values, intrinsics and passions and know how to harness them to create success. They have a keen sense of what they have and where it can take them. Visionaries "don't get caught up in the moment," Hiller told me. When setting a vision, they focus on the future and consider the possibilities.

Steve Jobs, founder of Apple Inc., is often referred to as a visionary because of his ability to imagine new ways of using technology to make life easier. Jobs has to imagine it, feel it, and own it before he can have his engineers create it. The same goes for you. You have to see and feel your potential success before you can start moving toward it.

Hiller, as a leadership researcher, believes that "vision is a self-created lens for defining the future and creating a sense of purpose." Creating a vision starts with thinking critically about what you want to accomplish, how it will look, and why you are going to do it. This requires pulling off the road, taking the keys out of the ignition, and looking under the hood to thoroughly check out what needs to be tended to before embarking on your journey. By visioning, you allow yourself to see the future happen. Some of you may do this by taking a vacation, meditating, or having a beer.

When I was a cross-country runner in high school, prior to every competition my coach had us lie down, close our eyes, and imagine running the race. As we lay there, he would gently talk us through the course. The idea was to get us to think about the terrain and the challenges. He wanted us to see what success would be like before we took a crack at it.

Every step you take in constructing and executing your YOU Plan should be checked and rechecked against your vision. Your vision is your guiding light. It should constantly remind you where you are going and why. In his most famous speech, the Rev. Dr. Martin Luther King Jr. began with the words, "I have a dream." His dream was a United States of America where skin color and ethnicity didn't matter – a dream toward which this nation continues to strive as it has made tremendous headway. Before King's work could begin, he had to have a vision.

CHOOSE YOUR ROLE MODELS

Role models make your vision and goals feel more real because you can see that they have been done before. They provide you with a template – a road map. This chapter's opening quote, from talk show host Chris Matthews (*Hardball* and *The Chris Matthews Show*), says we love biographies because they give us a road map. We can see in them the paths others have taken.

A role model personifies that which you seek. When seeking out a role model, look to people who have accomplished what you want. Be careful to examine their circumstances and how they differ from yours. You must be mindful that you are different and will need to forge your own way. Don't worry as much about following details of the person as following the spirit of what he or she represents. When choosing your role models, ask yourself:

- Who do I want to be like?

- Who would I like to be compared with?

- What is it that got them to where they are?

SET YOUR GOALS

Once you have a vision, think about the major life accomplishments you wish to attain. Think about what you need to accomplish to take charge of your career and get to your goal. There may be a variety of pathways to your vision, so figure out what makes the most sense for you.

When it comes to the value of goal setting, the research findings are clear: It works. Noted organizational psychologist Edwin Locke believes that setting goals is highly motivational because goals do three things: They focus your attention, keep you on track, and force you to strategize and plan.

Researchers tend to look at two types of goals: distal (long-range) and proximal (short-term). Think of distal goals as your major goals and proximal goals as your interim goals. You have to start with the larger, long-term view and then work on the interim goals required to get you there.

Your major goals may include working for a certain company, getting a specific job, starting on your own, or breaking into a new industry. Or you may be aiming for a promotion, degree or credential. Whatever your vision, you must consider what you need to accomplish to fulfill it.

A popular method for approaching goal setting is called SMART goals. Originating from the project management field, the concept has had a variety of interpretations. Typically, SMART goals are:

- **S**pecific – What exactly are you going to accomplish?

- **M**easurable – How will you know you accomplished it?

- **A**ttainable – Is the goal reasonably within your reach?

- **R**elevant – Does the specific goal fit in with your major goals and vision?

- **T**ime-bound – Do you have a schedule and deadlines?

CASE IN POINT:
KEEP A FINGER ON THE PULSE

Business and leadership guru John C. Maxwell believes in applying strategic thinking to every aspect of life. In his book How Successful Leaders Think, he outlines his own method for life and business planning:

"At the beginning of every month, I spend half a day working on my calendar for the next forty days." That prevents him from falling into the day-to-day planning trap. By scripting out his actions and keeping tabs on his progress, he always knows where he is and where he needs to be. "This strategy is one of the reasons I have been able to accomplish much," Maxwell says. For success, thoughtful planning and goal setting are priceless.

We all make lists and we all have calendars, the key is actually turning these lists and dates into concrete plans and committing to action.

Think of goals as way-points on your journey. Whether you are setting your major, longer-term goals or your shorter-term interim ones, using the SMART goal process as a guide will help. Stretch yourself a little. Researchers such as Locke have shown that making goals a little tougher will increase your likelihood for achievement. A major part of the YOU Plan process is challenging yourself and holding yourself accountable. It is time to start thinking about what it will take to get yourself out of the career hot seat and into the career game. SMART goals are a great technique for making this happen.

ORGANIZE YOUR GOALS

Author and entrepreneur Timothy Ferriss, known as an "ultravaga-bond" for his world sojourns, has a unique take on planning and goal setting, among other things. In his book *The 4-Hour Workweek*, Ferriss describes what he calls dreamlining, in which you put your dreams on paper and organize a plan to make them a reality. Although simple, the result is powerful. When you organize them on paper, Ferriss says, your "goals shift from ambiguous wants to defined steps." As most of us know, thinking about it is one thing; writing it down is another. At the outset of this book, I mentioned that ambiguity and uncertainty lead to stress. By planning, you take ambiguity away and give yourself a sense of control.

Since I was a 19-year-old sophomore at the University of Miami, my dream was to open my own private consulting practice as an organizational psychologist. To accomplish this major life goal, I knew I would have to pave the way by reaching other formidable goals. Those would include working for a major consulting firm and getting my doctorate in industrial and organizational psychology. Each of these major goals required hitting a number of interim goals.

Getting into a big firm meant demonstrating competence through internships and connections. It meant seeking out the right opportunities to set me up as a good candidate. Getting into a Ph.D. program meant building experience, researching schools, taking the GRE, and submitting lengthy applications. In and of themselves these are all significant feats, but they were also critical paths to attaining my larger goals. They were all steps in the plan.

CASE IN POINT:
KEEP BOTH HANDS ON THE WHEEL

Keith Ferrazzi, business consultant, marketing expert, and best-selling author of Never Eat Alone and Who's Got Your Back, says he uses a "personal success wheel" to keep on track. At the end of every year, he takes time off to reassess where he stands on seven major dimensions: deep relationships, professional growth, financial success, physical wellness, intellectual stimulation, spirituality, and giving back. The purpose is to ensure that his goals and actions are continuing to lead him toward the life he wants. By having a defined set of categories that he feels are of value in attaining success, Ferrazzi is able to ask himself the hard questions and hold himself to taking action.

If you want to own your destiny, you have to pick a direction and take the time to draw a road map for getting there.

Making connections: In the Intrinsics section, we discussed the value of leveraging relationships and affiliations. In setting your targets, ask yourself: What connections do I need to make?

Building competence: Ask yourself what skills, knowledge and abilities you need to further develop to better position yourself. What do you need to learn, and how are you going to go about learning it?

Getting credentials: Many fields have education or certification requirements that are important for recognition and advancement. You have to find out what these are and determine whether you need them. Professional associations and industry chat rooms are a good place to start.

Think about other types of interim goals. Keep in mind that applying the SMART goal method will help you better define these goals and keep you on track for achieving them.

DETERMINE YOUR ACTIVITIES

Picking a destination is one thing; getting there is another. A word I hear again and again from salespeople is *activity* – they know they have to be out there working to make things happen – and meeting your goals requires activity as well. Every plan has to be put into action. Knowing you have planned actions keeps you accountable. Here are some tips:

Make a list: If you really want to own it, write it down. Writing down your goals and activities (as I will ask you to do in the following chapter) is a great way to hold yourself accountable. Based on your major and interim goals, you need to come up with a list of activities that will get you there. You should be checking and revising this list every day.

Set a schedule: If you recall, part of the SMART goal method is setting deadlines. Sit down and schedule out your week, your month, and your year. Hold yourself accountable to deadlines, and do everything you can to meet them. Without deadlines, you will never achieve anything.

Market your brand: I spent a good portion of this book talking about how to articulate your essence and build your brand. Once you have developed your brand, you have to take it to market. Some suggestions of places to market your YOU Brand are:

- Networking events

- Social media

- Career fairs

- Professional associations

In marketing your brand, make sure to put your talking points to good use. Those sound bites you prepared will serve as guidelines for all of your branding activities.

PRIORITIZE YOUR ACTIVITIES

Unfortunately, you can't accomplish everything all at once. You have to decide where to start. Usually, that entails deciding what is most important, critical, time-sensitive or valuable. In other words, you have to prioritize or you will become paralyzed.

When prioritizing, keep in mind your larger career and life goals. For example, attaining financial success may require more intermediate goals that involve valuing something different. For example, you may take less money to get more prestige with the knowledge that the prestige will eventually get you the money. What you value at the moment depends on where you are in meeting your goals. That is why you have to understand your values, so you can set priorities according to your larger plan.

If you try to accomplish too much without a priority list, you fall back on doing what comes easiest or most naturally as opposed to furthering your cause. Whether you are a business leader or job seeker, prioritizing must be part of all your planning and execution. Priorities keep you on track and help you make consistent decisions.

A DR. WOODY MOMENT:
THE POWER OF PRIORITIZING

Often in my consulting, the obvious answer seems just beyond the view of my client. That phenomenon is quite normal. Because we are all victims of living in our own heads, we sometimes have to check in with an outsider.

One of the groups I was helping in a team exercise was struggling to get on track. They were hard-driving professionals, and their senior leader was even harder driving. They pursued nothing less than per-fection – but at a cost.

Their workload was intense and at times insurmountable. Their desire to do everything often led to committing too much and delivering too little. The result was an erratic and misaligned team where every-one prioritized by natural default. In other words, they went with the easy stuff first and worked to perfect it. This created a group of team members who all had different agendas, despite having the same roles and responsibilities.

The senior leader needed to align his goals to ensure that his efforts (and that of his team) supported the company's vision. He found himself with a team of individuals choosing to focus on what they were most comfortable with and doing way too much of it. His failure to set priorities and provide strong guidance caused misalign-ment across his team and gave his boss serious pause for concern. This ultimately came to a head, which is where I stepped in.

The key problem was his inability to pick his battles and direct the team on going forth and fighting those particular battles. You will never be able to win on all fronts. If you want success you have to be able to prioritize, which means you have to be willing to walk away from some fights.

The moral of this story is that without established priorities, you will never truly control your destiny. The stress and strain that results from a lack of direction will render you motionless. Pick your battles and do so enthusiastically.

CHOOSE YOUR MEASURES

If you don't measure, you don't know. As someone trained in the social sciences, I am constantly reminded that measurement is critical. To determine progress, you need to take relevant and accurate measurements, such as:

- The number of career leads generated

- The number of networking events attended

- The number of new connections made

- The number of contact meetings (coffees, lunches or cocktails)

- Number of targeted resumes sent out

- The number of first interviews

- Number of meetings with prospects or potential backers

The idea here is to set some simple targets and keep a tally. If you don't keep score, it will be tough to know how well you are doing in your career entrepreneur activities.

CHECK ON PROGRESS

Keeping such a tally will do you no good unless you look at it, and frequently. Noted author and sales guru Brian Tracy uses the term *return on energy* (ROE) – a variation of the business principle of *return on investment*. The idea is that in any venture, whether building a business or pursuing a career, you need to keep abreast of your progress.

The YOU Plan requires a serious investment of your time and energy. By checking your progress regularly, you are able to ensure that your efforts are bearing the results you want. If they are not, you can then adjust accordingly. It's likely that you check your gas gauge, bank statements, weight and cholesterol. If you are willing to check progress on those, you should also be willing to check progress on your career and life.

MAKE IT HAPPEN

The notion of taking it day-by-day is a failure mentality. It's a cop-out to avoid planning. Why don't we plan? We fear failure. So instead, we guarantee failure by wandering aimlessly and allowing our environment to guide us. Keep in mind, motion isn't progress, it's just motion. Without focus, it is nothing more than self-distraction. If you don't have a plan, you are a passenger. The YOU Plan is about making you a driver. The idea of being in the hot seat is about recognizing the reality of your situation as urgent, yet under your control. Getting out of the hot seat requires commitment and focus. It requires having a plan.

Keep in mind, you can plan your life away and never go anywhere. Don't be the talker who never takes action. This is where the rubber meets the road, so to speak. Don't be afraid. You have a plan, so get out and do it.

This chapter has provided you with a method for forging your own path. There is no one correct way to go about it. Do what feels right for you. Success and happiness are choices – your choices. Be ambitious, decide what you want, and work toward getting yourself out of the hot seat. Make a plan, and make it happen.

Chapter 13

CREATING YOUR YOU PLAN – EXERCISE VI

N ow that you have prioritized your VIPs, rediscovered your essence, and created a brand, it's time to put your work into action. It's time to take what you have done and create the YOU Plan.

STEP 1. STATE YOUR YOU VISION: In Exercise IV in Chapter 9, you articulated a vision based on your values, intrinsics and passions. It should be a simple statement describing what you are about. It should manifest your VIPs. Make sure it makes sense to you and those who know you well. Before moving on, restate that vision:

_____

_____

_____

_____

Does the vision you stated still make sense?   Yes ☐ No ☐
If no, go back and rethink it.

Do you have a passion for making this vision happen? Yes ☐ No ☐
If no, go back and rethink it.

STEP 2. **SPECIFY YOUR DIRECTION:** In Chapter 9, you also selected two potential career directions. Now, decide which one you really want to go after first. Prioritize them:

1)_____
2)_____

Considering your top priority direction, what type of career do you really want to build? Outline your number one career direction.

_____

_____

_____

_____

What will you call yourself? What is your name for your career, role, position, vocation? (Be creative; this is yours, so own it.)

_____

_____

_____

_____

Who do you want to work with?

_____

_____

_____

_____

What does success look like? Ideally, what will be your role, and what will your career and life look like? Consider level of responsibility, type of contributions, your stature and profile, and the possibilities open to you.

_____

_____

_____

_____

_____

_____

STEP 3. IDENTIFY YOUR ROLE MODELS

Who has successfully done what you want to accomplish?

_____

_____

_____

_____

Why are they your role models?

_____

_____

_____

_____

What do they have in common? Is there a theme to how they achieved success? What can you learn form them?

_____

_____

_____

_____

STEP 4. SET YOUR MAJOR GOALS: To accomplish your vision and build a YOU Plan, you have to set goals. As discussed in the last chapter, they should be SMART goals that are Simple, Measurable, Attainable, Relevant, and Time-bound. List the major goals that will be critical in attaining your selected career direction:

1) _____

2) _____

3) _____

4) _____

5) _____

STEP 5. IDENTIFY YOUR INTERIM GOALS: To attain your major goals, you first need to reach interim goals – short-term goals that are critical to your long-term ones. For each major goal, list the interim goals that will be necessary in moving the ball forward on attaining your larger goals (again, consider the SMART principle):

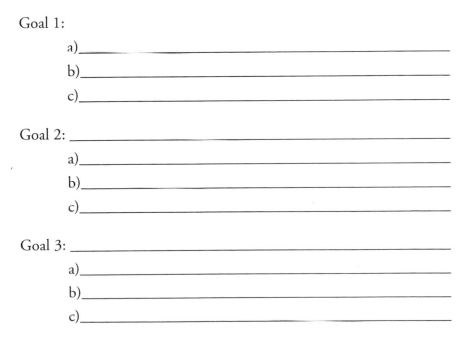

Goal 1:

    a) _____

    b) _____

    c) _____

Goal 2: _____

    a) _____

    b) _____

    c) _____

Goal 3: _____

    a) _____

    b) _____

    c) _____

Goal 4: _____

    a)_____

    b)_____

    c)_____

Goal 5: _____

    a)_____

    b)_____

    c)_____

STEP 6. DECIDE ON CRITICAL ACTIVITIES: Activities are how you bring your goals to fruition. Take the time to make a list of activities, prioritize them, and set a schedule for getting them done. For downloadable activity charts for this section, go to www.TheYOUPlan. com.

Ask yourself, what are the things I actually need to do on a daily, weekly, and monthly basis? Think about the specific actions that will help you meet your interim/short-term goals.

Daily activities (what should I be doing every day?):

_____

_____

_____

_____

Weekly activities (what should I be doing every week?):

_____

_____

_____

_____

Monthly activities (what should I be doing every month?):

_____

_____

_____

_____

STEP 7. SELECT AND PRIORITIZE
YOUR CRITICAL ACTIVITIES:

To get yourself started, select 10 activities that will get you moving towards your identified goals and commit to some timelines for getting them done. Go back to your VIPs and think about the relationships you need to build, the skills you need to polish, or the brand development you need to focus on.

Activity   *Completion date*

1) _____   _____/_____/_____

2) _____   _____/_____/_____

3) _____   _____/_____/_____

4) _____   _____/_____/_____

5) _____   _____/_____/_____

6) _____   _____/_____/_____

7) _____   _____/_____/_____

8) _____   _____/_____/_____

9) _____   _____/_____/_____

10) _____   _____/_____/_____

STEP 8. CHOOSE YOUR MEASURES: To gauge accomplishment, you have to measure progress through means that you can control, as discussed in the previous chapter. What types of tangible measures will help you determine progress on your major goals?

1) _____

2) _____

3) _____

4) _____

5) _____

STEP 9. CREATE THE YOU PLAN: Put it all together and get it done! Now that you have put in the time and answered the questions, it's time to lay out your YOU Plan. Go to www.TheYouPlan.com and download (or print out) the YOU Plan spreadsheet to create a simple straightforward YOU Plan based on the answers to the exercises in this book.

Chapter 14

DON'T GO IT ALONE

"He that teaches himself hath a fool for a master."
– BENJAMIN FRANKLIN

D on't ever be too proud to seek out help or ask for feedback. Successful people marshal their resources. I want to share some thoughts on putting together your team and seeking out some interesting ways to get support from others.

FIND A MENTOR

Mentoring is an age-old concept. History is filled with stories of sages, masters, confidants and tutors. Plato had Aristotle, Oprah Winfrey had Maya Angelou, Jay Leno had Johnny Carson, and Luke Skywalker had Obi-Wan Kenobi.

Many craft and trade fields still require apprenticeships, and a good number of Fortune 500 companies have formal mentoring programs for professional staff. When I took my first job at PricewaterhouseCoopers Consulting, I was assigned a mentor. Later in my career I sought out my own mentors.

Great mentors typically had their own mentors and appreciate the process. Look for a mentor who does what you want to do, who lives the life you want to have, and, most importantly, shares your values. Find someone who cares about you, is willing to dedicate the time you need, and genuinely wants to help you succeed.

CREATE A SUPPORT GROUP

You are not alone. If you feel alone, it's because you choose to be alone. A lot of people are going through the same experience as you – feeling the same feelings, running up against the same walls, fighting the same fights. There are a lot of folks out there sitting in the hot seat. They are feeling the heat from the pressure to get out and make something happen. To find them, you have to want to find them. And you have to be willing to share. A strong support system is vital to living a good life. Creating a support group can be a great way to really get engaged in your career planning.

Support groups come in many shapes and sizes. A support group can be a network of friends who meet weekly over coffee to share challenges and offer perspectives. Or it can be a professionally facilitated group discussion led by a career coach, with structured sharing sessions and goal-setting activities. It can be a group of like-minded professionals all seeking to get ahead or learn from one another.

Whatever shape a support group takes, the focus must be on progress. Those who lash out, blame, or validate failure are not offering you support. They're enabling you to feel victimized and allowing you to relinquish accountability. Support is about helping one another, not commiserating.

We all learn from our interactions. It's nice to know you aren't alone, and it helps to hear how others have dealt with career transitions. In his best-seller *Who's Got Your Back*, Keith Ferrazzi focuses on the critical role that support systems play in attaining success. Ferrazzi talks about developing "lifeline relationships," which he defines as your inner circle of confidants and advisers you turn to during pivotal junctures in your life. Having those go-to friends can be a great advantage.

Being a career entrepreneur can require learning a new business, redirecting your energies, finding a need, and creating a position for yourself. To do those things, you need to learn from others. Find people in the know who are willing to provide the support you need to get yourself out of the hot seat and back on a serious career track.

Chapter 15

THE PATH AHEAD

"Preparation, I have often said, is rightly two-thirds of any venture."
— Amelia Earhart

I'll never forget a chat I had with my grandfather, a lifelong golfer who had a 7 handicap in his prime. One day, tired of swinging like an ax murderer on the range, I decided to hit the putting green for a while. I tried to keep control but consistently came up short of the hole. At dinner, I complained to my grandfather that I always under-hit my putts. Slightly amused, he looked at me and said simply: "You'll never make a putt if you don't try to reach the hole." Bottom line: If you aim short you will come up short.

In *The Prince*, the oft-maligned Niccolo Machiavelli talks about the role of thoughtful and deliberate action:

> *"He should act like a prudent archer who, knowing the limitation of his bow and judging the target to be too far off, sets his aim still farther off, not to strike so distant a mark, but rather to strike the desired target through the more ambitious aim."*

Whether you are just graduating or are a seasoned professional back on the hunt, you are the archer. You choose your path. You set the goals. You plan the activities. Achieving success is on you and no one else. Every day I come across blamers and victims who spend their energy pointing the finger and creating excuses for their failures. If you want to thrive in the new economy, you can't be a blamer. You have to be a planner.

Coaches have game plans, teachers have lesson plans, pilots have flight plans, CEOs have business plans – and successful people have career plans. Without a YOU Plan, you are not in control. Without a YOU Plan, you are at the mercy of those around you. Without a YOU Plan, you are a follower. No one cares more about you than you. Take responsibility for yourself and your own success. Don't wait for the government to bail you out or for some good Samaritan to rescue you. You are the solution.

By now you know this book isn't about rewriting your resume or learning to regurgitate canned answers to bad interviewers. It's not a book of tips on where to find your next job or how to surf job boards. That's all been done, redone, and overdone. Some of those books can be helpful, and I encourage you to use them – when you are ready.

Nor is the point of this book to get you to revisit childhood fantasies. Rather, it's about rediscovering your true passions, making a plan to fulfill them, and taking control of your destiny during uncertain times. It's about stepping back, using your head, and getting yourself out of the hot seat. It's about creating The YOU Plan.

I'd like to leave you with this final thought: Live life deliberately, seek out inspiration, and enjoy the journey. It's all up to you!

Thank you for your time, and congratulations. You have taken a serious step toward owning your career destiny. And if you go to www.TheYouPlan.com, you can access a lot of free information and check out the planning tool for a more electronic approach to planning. With such tools in hand and determination in mind, you are on your way to being a true career entrepreneur.

Please feel free to send me any feedback you may have on the book or the website. Also, if you have a great YOU Plan story, please drop me a line. I look forward to hearing from you. You can contact me at:

www.TheYouPlan.com

Or

www.DrWoody.com

About the Author

Michael "Dr. Woody" Woodward, Ph.D., is a CEC-certified professional coach and consultant trained in organizational psychology. He works with private and corporate clients on career development and improving management and leadership. As an author and speaker, he focuses on career psychology in the new economy and on developing management and executive leadership.

Dr. Woody is president of the Miami-based consulting firm Human Capital Integrated (HCI), which he founded in 2005. The firm focuses on management and leadership development. He also is the founder of DrWoody.com, a dynamic media site dedicated to work-life issues and career entrepreneurialism in the new economy. He serves on the academic advisory board for the Florida International University Center for Leadership.

Before founding his consulting firm, Dr. Woody was a management and human resources consultant for PricewaterhouseCoopers Consulting (PwC) and a project manager for IBM Business Consulting Services in Washington, D.C.

Dr. Woody received a bachelor's degree in psychology from the University of Miami, a master's degree in industrial and organizational psychology from Springfield College, and a PhD in industrial and organizational psychology from Florida International University.

Speaking and Workshops

Dr. Woody works with individuals and organizations on personal and professional development. He is also available for keynote speaking, workshops and consultation. To find out more about Dr. Woody, go to: www.DrWoody.com

Dr. Woody in the media: Dr. Woody has appeared on the Bravo Network's Tabatha's Salon Takeover as a guest expert working with Tabatha and her team. Dr. Woody has also appeared on the *CBS-4 Miami Evening News, Focus on South Florida, The Herald Business Show, and 880 The Bizz*. Dr. Woody has been quoted in the *Miami Herald, Miami Today, the South Florida Sun Sentinel, Miami Monthly,* and *Miami Magazine* as an expert on career re-engagement. From 2007 to 2009, Dr. Woody wrote a regular column for *Go Jobing* magazine on issues around hiring and coaching. Dr. Woody has also published award-winning research on teamwork titled *Cooperation and Competition: The Effects of Team Entrainment and Reward Structure* (Woodward, Randall, Price, and Saravia, 2005).

TreeNeutral™

Advantage Media Group is proud to be a part of the Tree Neutral™ program. Tree Neutral offsets the number of trees consumed in the production and printing of this book by taking proactive steps such as planting trees in direct proportion to the number of trees used to print books. To learn more about Tree Neutral, please visit **www.treeneutral. com.** To learn more about Advantage Media Group's commitment to being a responsible steward of the environment, please visit **www. advantagefamily.com/green**

The YOU Plan is available in bulk quantities at special discounts for corporate, institutional, and educational purposes. To learn more about the special programs Advantage Media Group offers, please visit **www.KaizenUniversity.com** or call 1.866.775.1696.

Advantage Media Group is a leading publisher of business, motivation, and self-help authors. Do you have a manuscript or book idea that you would like to have considered for publication? Please visit **www.amgbook.com**

LaVergne, TN USA
19 April 2010
179762LV00004B/114/P